First Edition

Genuine **A**utographed **C**ollectible

Do you want me to sign it in ink or in lipstick?

Gift Card

Date:

To:

From:

Message:

What Do Books Do?
BOOKS ARE POWERFUL!

Books **Educate!**
Books **Enlighten!**
Books **Empower!**
Books **Emancipate!**
Books **Entertain!**
Books **Spring** Eternal!
Books **Drive** Exploration!
Books **Spark** Evolution!
Books **Ignite** Revolution!

SHARON ESTHER LAMPERT

Gift Shop: BooksArePowerful.com

V.E.S.S.E.L.
Very. Extra. Special. Sharon. Esther. Lampert.

KADIMAH PRESS
Gifts of Genius

Literature, Poetry, Education, Creativity, Genius, Sharon Esther Lampert

V.E.S.S.E.L. Very. Extra. Special. Sharon. Esther. Lampert.
SEE THE WORLD THROUGH THE EYES OF A CREATIVE GENIUS

©2022 by Sharon Esther Lampert. All Rights Reserved.
No part of this book may be used or reproduced in any manner whatsoever without written permission except in the case of brief quotations embodied in critical articles and reviews.

KADIMAH PRESS: GIFTS OF GENIUS
Books may be purchased for education, business, or sales promotional use.

ISBN Hardcover: 978-1-885872-09-8
ISBN Paperback: 978-1-885872-10-4
ISBN E-Book: 978-1-885872-11-1
Library of Congress Control Number: 2022915694

Fan Mail:
Website: www.SharonEstherLampert.com
Email: FANS@SharonEstherLampert.com

For Global Online Orders and Distribution:
INGRAM 1 Ingram Blvd. La Vergne, TN 37086-3629
Phone: 615-793-5000, Fax orders: 615-287-6990

Age 9
THE QUEEN HAS ARRIVED!
"My daughter is a poet, philosopher, and teacher.
She is the Princess & the Pea!
BEAUTY & BRAINS!"
MOMMY
XOXO

LOVE OF MY LIFETIME: MOMMY EVE PAIKOFF LAMPERT

Book Design and Interior: Prodigy Sharon Esther Lampert

Editor: Dave Segal

First Edition

Manufactured in the United States of America

Dedication

MOMMY
Who Knew Who I Was From the **INSIDE OUT** at Age 9

"**One great poem** is lucky.
Two great poems mean I have something,
but I don't know what it is.
Three great poems mean I have something,
and I have to learn to work it—but there is
no instruction manual.
Four great poems mean I have a gift,
and the gift is a mystery."
—Sharon Esther Lampert

LITERATURE IS POWERFUL BEYOND WORDS FOR IT CREATES WORLDS

Sharon Esther Lampert
Poet, Prophet, Philosopher, Peacemaker, Paladin of Education, Prodigy

SEE THE WORLD THROUGH THE EYES OF A CREATIVE GENIUS

EIGHTEEN POETRY BOOKS
3 Editions: Hardcover, Paperback, and E-Book

The Greatest Poems Ever Written on Extraordinary World Events

1. I Stole All the Words From The Dictionary
2. **IMMORTALITY IS MINE**: Greatest Poems Ever Written on Extraordinary World Events
3. **POETRY JEWELS:** **D**iamonds, **E**meralds, **S**apphires, **R**ubies, and **P**earls
4. **V.E.S.S.E.L.** **V**ery. **E**xtra. **S**pecial. **S**haron. **E**sther. **L**ampert.
5. Does Your Kid Read Sharon Esther Lampert?
6. Does Your Professor Teach Reason-N-Rhyme?
7. What Happens When You Dress Up Albert Einstein as Marilyn Monroe?
8. Sharon Esther Lampert: The Sexiest Creative Genius in Human History
9. **SEA IN, SEE OUT:** Childhood Poem
10. **CUPID:** Language of Love — Written in Letter C
11. Spiraling Downward, Upward We Stand United: 911 World Trade Center Tragedy
12. In 5 Minutes, Learn 5000 Years of Jewish History
13. Love Ever Reborn Is Love Ever Newborn
14. It's Not Easy Being a JEWISH SEX SYMBOL But Someone Has to Do It!
    Poems Written About Sharon Esther Lampert by Her Fans
15. **SWEET NOTHINGS:** Love Portraits in Poetry
16. Witches, Whores, Wives, and Writers (Feminist Poems)
17. No **F**akes! No **F**lops! No **F**illers! No **F**at! No **F**-Bomb!
18. 7 Practice Husbands: Love Portraits in Poetry

• Buy Autographed Books Online

• All Global Bookstores: USA, CAN, UK, AUS, ASIA, AFRICA, INDIA and MIDDLE EAST

Table of Contents

POPULAR POEMS
- POETREE ... p. 1
- THE 22 COMMANDMENTS ... pp. 2-3
- WORLD PEACE EQUATION ... p. 4
- TRUE LOVE ... p. 5
- BE ART ... p. 9
- BE BORN ... p. 10
- EDUCATE NOT ... p. 11
- IMPOSSIBLE ... p. 12
- What Other People Think ... p. 13
- FINITE ... p. 14
- DEADICATION ... p. 15

- How to Read a Poem by Sharon Esther Lampert ... p. 7
- 10 Poetry Reading Tips ... p. 19

WORLD POETRY RECORD Eve is Liberated from 5000 Years of Misogyny
- **WORLD POETRY RECORD: 120 Words of Rhyme from One Family of Rhyme Through the Eyes of Eve (rhyme)** ... pp. 16-18

POET'S FAVORITE POEMS
- Haiti Earthquake: Crimes of Insanity Against Humanity ... p. 20
- TSUNAMI ... p. 21
- The Militant Palestinian Toddler Terrorist ... p. 22
- Carmel Forest Fires: Wherever Israelis Go, Gardens Grow ... p. 23

THE GREATEST POEMS EVER WRITTEN ON EXTRAORDINARY WORLD EVENTS
GLOBAL CATASTROPIC TRAUMA (poetryessentialservice.com)
- COVID19: The World We Left Behind ... pp. 24-25

JEWISH HOLOCAUST POEMS
Mandatory Holocaust Education (poetryjewels.com)
- Carmel Forest Fires: Wherever Israelis Go, Gardens Grow ... p. 23
- Simon Wiesenthal: Nazi Hunter ... pp. 44-45
- Casting Light: Our Sister Edith Stein of the Star of David ... pp. 46-47

BLACK LIVES MATTER POEMS
Poetry Reading at Epenezer Baptist Church Boca Raton, Florida
- Nelson Mandela THE DELIVERER ... p. 40
- Dr. Martin Luther King Jr. THE DELIVERER ... pp. 41-43

KADIMAH PRESS: Gifts of Genius

Sharon Esther Lampert's **BIG BRAIN** Conceptualizes
BIG IDEAS Using One Letter of the Alphabet

What Do Books Do?
—Written in Letter **E**

Seven Goalposts of Education
—Written in Letter **E**

Sharon Esther's Biography
—Written in Letters **F, B** and **P**

CUPID
The Language of Love
—Written in Letter **C**

Make Life Make Sense

TEMPORARY INSANITY
We Are All Building Our Lives on a **S**and Trap
—Written in Letter **S**

THE SECRET SAUCE OF BOOK SALES
How to Make Money Selling Books
—Written in Letter **P**

DESTINY
Are You Living Your Life By Default or by Design?
—Written in Letter **D**

WIN AT THIN
FAT ME to SKINNY ME
What Works What Doesn't Work
This Book Changed My Life!
—Written in Letter **A**

FEMINISM POEMS
- TRUE LOVE ... p. 4
- Through The Eyes of Eve WORLD POETRY RECORD (rhyme) ... pp. 16-18
- MINUS ZERO WOMAN ... p. 32
- STOP CAMPUS RAPE (2016) ... p. 33
- Central Park Violence Against Women: Water Fight, Flight, and Tears ... pp. 34-35 (The Most Published Poem on the Internet)
- Fisted Rose Publication ... pp. 38-39
- Casting Light: Our Sister Edith Stein of the Star of David ... pp. 46-47

EPIC POEMS
- EPIC: 911 Spiraling Downward, Upward We Stand United ... pp. 26-31
- EPIC: In 5 Minutes, Learn 5000 Years of Jewish History ... pp. 48-49
- EPIC: Love Ever Reborn Is Love Ever Newborn ... pp. 57-61

STAND-UP COMEDY
- SAFE SEX — Dr. C. Silk ... p. 50
- Dating a Gynecologist — Dr. B. Ginsberg ... p. 51

LOVE POEMS
- TRUE LOVE ... p. 4
- First Love ... p. 52
- That Kiss ... (rhyme) p. 53
- CUPID: The Mating Season ... p. 54
- My Man ... p. 55
- REMO: Drink, Drink, Drink ... (rhyme) p. 56
- EPIC: Love Ever Reborn Is Love Ever Newborn ... pp. 57-61

SEE THE WORLD THOUGH THE EYES OF A CREATIVE GENIUS
- About Sharon Esther Lampert ... pp. 62-66
- One of the World's Greatest Poets ... p. 67
- SEXIEST CREATIVE GENIUS IN HUMAN HISTORY ... pp. 70-71, 73, 79
- FAN MAIL ... pp. 69-79
- National and International Poetry Publications ... pp. 80-81
- WORLD FAMOUS QUOTES ... pp. 82-83
- KADIMAH PRESS: Gifts of Genius ... pp. 84-85
- Count Your Blessings. Practice Gratitude ... p. 86

SEE THE WORLD THROUGH THE

SHARON ESTHER LAMPERT

The Greatest Poems Ever Written on Extraordinary World Events

EYES OF A CREATIVE GENIUS

WARNING

KEEP A SAFE DISTANCE OF 6 FEET

HIGH LEVELS OF INTENSITY

INTELLECTUAL COMBUSTION

SHARON ESTHER LAMPERT

PRODIGY

POET, PHILOSOPHER, PROPHET, PEACEMAKER,
PALADIN OF EDUCATION, PHOTON SUPERHERO
PIONEER, PERFORMER, PUBLISHER, PLAYER
PRESIDENT, PHOENIX, PRINCESS of ISRAEL

"The Sole Intention of My Poetry is to Add LIGHT to Your Soul"

"Food is for the Body
Education is for the Mind
Poetry is for the Soul"

"I AM an OPEN Book, to KNOW ME is to READ ME"

"Every Thought in Your Head Was Put There by a Writer"

"When I'm not Writing I'm Reading. When I'm not Writing or Reading, I'm Singing."

"Please Don't Let Me Die with a Typo!"

POE**T**REE

Ink needs a Pen
Pen needs Paper
Paper needs a Poem
Poem needs a Poet
Poet needs a Muse
Muse needs a Poet
Poet needs Divine Inspiration
Divine Inspiration needs Divine Intervention
Divine Intervention needs Divine Grace
Divine Grace needs Immortality
Immortality needs Eternity
Eternity needs Readers of Poetry

By Sharon Esther Lampert

@All Rights Reserved. Sharon Esther Lampert.

YOU HAD TO OUTDO MOSES!

Moses Has 10 Commandments. You Have 22 Commandments!

— Joel Rapplefeld

SHARON ESTHER LAMPERT
8TH PROPHETESS OF ISRAEL

The 8 Prophetesses of Israel

Sarah
Ageless Beauty, Seer, Holy Spirit
- Genesis 17:15-17:27
- Genesis 18:1-18:15
- Genesis 21:1-21:22
- Genesis 23:1-23:20

Miriam
Saved the life of Moses
- Exodus 2:1-2:10
- Exodus 15:20-15:27
- Numbers 12:1-12:16
- Numbers 20:1-20:6

Deborah
Warrior and 4th Judge
- Judges 4:4-4:14
- Judges 5:1-5:31

Hannah
Personal Prayer
- 1 Samuel 1:1-1:28

Abigail
Prophecy of King David
- 1 Samuel 25:2-25:44
- 1 Samuel 27:1-27:3
- 1 Samuel 30:4
- 2 Samuel 2:2
- 2 Samuel 3:2

Huldah
Learning, Enlightenment, and Peace
- 2 Kings 22:1-20

Esther
Rescued Jews from Genocide
- Esther 2:7-2:23
- Esther 4:1-4:16
- Esther 5:1-5:8
- Esther 7:1-7:10
- Esther 8:3-8:8
- Esther 9:12-9:14
- Esther 9:26-9:32

Sharon Esther Lampert
- 22 Commandments
- World Peace Equation
- 40 Absolute Truths
- World Poetry Record
- 40 Universal Gold Standards of Education
- 22 Steps to Find a Soulmate
- 10 Thinking Tools of Creative Genius

All You Will Ever Need to Know About God
The 22 Commandments
A Universal Moral Compass For All People, For All Religions, and For All Time

1. **LIFE** Over Death
2. **STRENGTH** Over Weakness
3. **DEED** Over Sin
4. **LOVE** Over Hatred
5. **TRUTH** Over Lie
6. **WISDOM** Over Stupidity
7. **OPTIMISM** Over Pessimism
8. **SHARING** Over Selfishness
9. **PRAISE** Over Criticism
10. **LOYALTY** Over Abandonment
11. **RESPONSIBILITY** Over Blame
12. **GRATITUDE** Over Envy
13. **REWARD** Over Punishment
14. **DEMOCRACY** Over Domination
15. **CREATION** Over Destruction
16. **EDUCATION** Over Ignorance
17. **COOPERATION** Over Competition
18. **FREEDOM** Over Oppression
19. **COMPASSION** Over Indifference
20. **FORGIVENESS** Over Revenge
21. **PEACE** Over War
22. **JOY** Over Suffering

"Moses had 10 commandments. You have 22 commandments. You had to out do Moses."
Joel Rapplefeld

"Inside Every Jewish Person Is a Little Moses Tying to Get Out"
Chabad Rabbi Ben Tzion Krasnianski

Sharon Esther Lampert
KADIMAH
8TH Prophetess of Israel

Learn It. Live It. Share It.

---

1. Sarah: (Genesis 21:12) Ageless Beauty, Seer, Holy Spirit
2. Miriam: Exodus 15:21 Saved the life of Moses
3. Devorah: Judges 4:4 Warrior and 4th Judge
4. Chanah: I Samuel 2:1-10 Personal Prayer
5. Abigail: I Samuel (25:2-44) Prophecy of King David
6. Huldah: Kings 22:14 Learning, Enlightenment, and Peace
7. Esther: The Book of Esther Saved the Jews from Genocide
8. Kadimah: 22 Commandments Beauty, Seer, Holy Spirit, Learning, Engli

@All Rights Reserved. Sharon Esther Lampert.

#1 Poetry Website for Student Projects

WORLD PEACE EQUATION

$VG + VL = VP$

Virtue of the Good + Value of Life = Vision of Peace

The Mathematical and Philosophical Proof for World Peace

$$VG + VL = VP$$
$$VP = VG + VL$$
$$VP = V(G+L)$$
$$P = (G+L)$$

Peace = Good + Life

Peace = Good Life

www.WorldPeaceEquation.com

@All Rights Reserved. Sharon Esther Lampert.

#1 Poetry Website for Student Projects

True Love

True Love is Unconditional.
True Love is Found in the Deed.
True Love is Found in the We.
True Love Joins the Heart,
Mind, and Body as One.

By Sharon Esther Lampert

My gifts did not come with an instruction manual. There were no teachers to guide me, and no classes to teach how to maximize my creative potential. I am its servant and messenger, and the instrument of its desires and destiny!

Sharon Esther Lampert

Poet
Prophet
Philosopher
Paladin of Education
Peacemaker
Princess Kadimah
Prodigy
PINUP

How to Read a Poem by Sharon Esther Lampert

1. Sharon's Poetry Paintings
Similar to the poet William Blake, her poems are accompanied by elaborate visual graphics that enrich and compliment the text. The poems are wall hangings, and her poems are framed by ardent fans and hang in their living spaces, like paintings. Students, the world over, read her poems in their classrooms, and use her poetry for their school assignments.

2. Sharon is a Master of Condensation
Sharon is a master of the art of condensation. She is able to condense a major world event in world history into a one-page poem. Her immortal literary gems come in a variety of lengths: A single sentence, a single page, and grand sweeping epics.

3. Sharon Is a Literary Photographer
Her poems are telescopic of the main event and microscopic of the infinite details.

4. Sharon Can Pack a Single Verse
Sharon's poems are known for her ability to weave poetry, philosophy, and comedy into a single verse.

5. Documentary Poet: Poems are Cinematic Journey's Through History
Sharon's poems take you on a cinematic journey, and make you feel as if you are reliving the event, as if it happened today.

6. Sharon's Poems Are Completed Literary Works
Many poets leave abandoned poems that went unfinished. Sharon's poems are completed works of art. Every word is essential to the poem. You cannot remove or replace a word. There are no extra words. Every word has its rightful place and fits to perfection.

7. Sharon's Poems Are All Inspired Works of Art
All of her poems are inspired. There are no rough drafts. Like giving birth to a baby, the poem incubates in her extra-body part a "Creative Apparatus" and is birthed in minutes. Like a baby, the poems are delivered whole and complete.

8. Sharon's Signature Endings: The Epiphany (Spiritual Illumination)
Quote: "The Sole Intention of My Poetry Is to Add LIGHT to Your Soul"
The last verse of every poem delivers a message that educates, enlightens, and empowers. Her searing signature endings find their way into your heart, open your mind to a deeper understanding, and stay with you forever.

©2000. All Rights Reserved. Sharon Esther Lampert.
FAN MAIL: FANS@SharonEstherLampert.com

BE ART

ART IS SMART
ART IS OF THE HEART
MAKE ART NOT WAR
YOU ARE BORN FOR GREATNESS
YOR ARE A MASTERPIECE

SHARON ESTHER LAMPERT
www.sharonestherlampert.com

Gift Shop: ArtHeart.store

#1 Poetry Website for Student Projects

BE BORN

Find the Light and Live in the Light!

Be Born.
Become Educated.
Love Your Work.
Make a Meaningful Contribution—
to Yourself, Your Family, and Humanity.
Be a True Friend to Yourself First.
Have Sex with Someone You Love.
Make Love with Complete Abandon.
Enjoy Unconditional Love from Your Devoted Pet.
Make Time to Read the Funnies and Laugh.
Save Enough Money to Visit the Popular,
Pretty, and Peaceful Places of the World.
Read Great Literature, Listen to Great Music,
See Great Art, Watch the Great Movies,
Play the Fun Sports, and Dance till Dawn.
Taste the Great Culinary Delights of the World—
Eat Slowly, Enjoy Every Bite, and Stay in Shape.
Plan One Great Adventure and Stick to the Plan.
Grow Old and Wise.
Leave Your Money to Someone
You Love—Who Loves You Back.
Die in Your Sleep.

By Sharon Esther Lampert

@All Rights Reserved. Sharon Esther Lampert.

#1 Poetry Website for Student Projects

EDUCATE NOT

No Time to Teach:
In Class, They Give a General Overview.
On Tests, They Want Particular Details.

No Time to Learn:
All By Myself, I Got to Teach Myself a Zillion Facts:
I Got No Study Skills, I Got No Tutor,
The First Day of School, I Gotta Be Behind.

Students Got a Cheat-Sheet:
I Use Citations From Books
I Got No Time to Read.

Teachers Got a Cheat Sheet:
They Got No Time to Read IT.
They Weigh IT:
Looks Beautiful
They Grade IT A.
Looks Pretty
They Grade IT B.
Looks OK
They Grade IT C.
Looks Ugly
They Grade IT D.
Looks Can Kill
They Grade IT F.

Quantity Over Quality:
Education System is Dumb
And is Gonna Get Dumber,
Wastes My Good Dime,
My Good Mind,
And My Good Time.
I Survive, I Don't Thrive.

Facts Move From Textbook
To Blackboard to Notebook.
Gotta Get the Facts **INSIDE OF ME:**
No Time to Think,
No Time to Write an Outline,
No Time for Research,
No Time to Write a Rough Draft,
No Time to Reread, Revise, and Rewrite,
No Time to Write a Final Draft,
No Time to Write My Masterpiece.
When I Get IT Back, My Work-In-Progress,
I Trash IT. I Got No Time for Junk.

Teachers Got No Time to Teach.
I Got No Time to Learn.
No Time to Educate.
EDUCATE NOT.

By Sharon Esther Lampert
Creative Genius
www.WorldFamousPoems.com

#1 Poetry Website for Student Projects

April 30: NYC Poetry in Pocket Day

IMPOSSIBLE

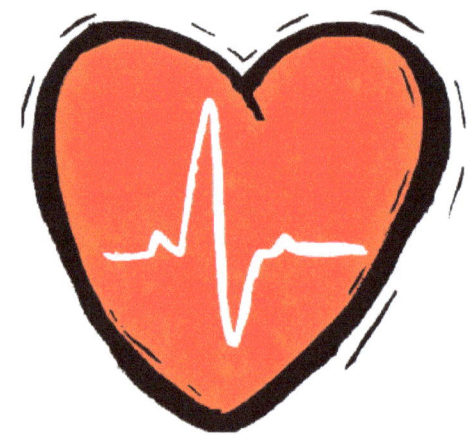

It is impossible to breathe in air,

Without breathing in toxic pollutants.

It is impossible to eat nutritious food,

Without ingesting chemicals and preservatives.

It is impossible to have a loving relationship,

Without bumping into a loved one's emotional problems.

And it is impossible not to breathe, eat, and love.

Sharon Esther Lampert

#1 Poetry Website for Student Projects

April 30: NYC Poetry in Pocket Day

What Other People Think

People who want to like you

will find something to like about you.

These people are called your **Friends.**

People who don't want to like you

will find something not to like about you.

These people are called your **Critics.**

People who don't want to like you

but can't find something about you

not to like will make something up.

These people are called your **Enemies.**

Sharon Esther Lampert

The Sole Intention of My Poetry Is to Add **LIGHT** to Your Soul

#1 Poetry Website for Student Projects

April 30: NYC Poetry in Pocket Day

FINITE

Days live and die.

Suns rise and set.

Flowers bloom and wither.

Fruits ripen and spoil.

Ice cream freezes and melts.

Candles shed light and darken.

Energies are generated and depleted.

Monies are made and spent.

Time is used and squandered.

Love burns eternal and passions wane.

Lives are breathed and become breathless.

Sharon Esther Lampert
The Sole Intention of My Poetry Is to Add **LIGHT** to Your Soul

#1 Poetry Website for Student Projects

April 30: NYC Poetry in Pocket Day

DEADICATION

Every single second of the day,

A suffering is taking place:

Shake-Me. Wake-Me. Save Me.

Every single second of the day,

My belief in a God is shaken:

Shake-Me. Wake-Me. Save Me.

GOD IS DEAD.

Sharon Esther Lampert

The Sole Intention of My Poetry Is to Add **LIGHT** to Your Soul

POETRY WORLD RECORD

Bibical Eve is Given a Voice, and Liberated from 5000 Years of Misogyny

1. It is a Poetry World Record of 120 words of rhyme from one family of rhyme.
2. It is an unchallengeable literary feat by a woman never before done by a man.
3. Every single verse has poetry, philosophy, and comedy.
4. The poem travels a long distance, from the birth of Adam to the present moment.
5. I gave Eve, the first woman of the Bible a voice, and liberated her from 5000 years of mysogyny. **Someone had to do it!**
6. Philosophy: In each stanza, there is a **known** and **unknown**.
7. The structure of the poem follows the exact format of the verses from the Bible.

Genesis 2:18-23	
Genesis 2:16	Stanza One: Gift of Eve
Geneis 3:1-5	Stanza Two: Forbidden Fruit
Genesis 3:6	Stanza Three: Eve's Gift
Genesis 3:20	Stanza Four: Serpent
Genesis 3:6	Stanza Five: Adam Eats Fruit
Genesis 3-12	Stanza Six: Adam Blames Eve
Genesis 3:17-19	Stanza Seven: The Exile
Genesis 3:23	Stanza Eight: Eve's Gift of Childbirth
Genesis 3:16	Stanza Nine: Adam and Eve's Gift (SEX)
Genesis 4:1	Stanza Ten: Future Generations
Genesis 5:1	

120 Words of Rhyme From One Family of Rhyme

#1 Poetry Website for Student Projects

THE GREATEST POEM EVER WRITTEN ON EVE
POETRY WORLD RECORD
120 WORDS OF RHYME FROM ONE FAMILY OF RHYME
EVERY VERSE HAS POETRY, PHILOSOPHY, AND COMEDY
AN UNCHALLENGEABLE LITERARY FEAT BY A WOMAN
AN UNCHALLENGEABLE LITERARY FEAT FOR ALL EONS
POEMS TRAVELS FROM CREATION TO PRESENT MOMENT
EVE LIBERATED FROM 5000 YEARS OF MISOGYNY

Through the Eyes of Eve
GOD Gave Adam the Gift of Eve (Genesis 2:18);
GOD Gave Eve the Gift of Life (Genesis 2:20).

Foreshown
GOD **Knowingly** gave to Adam
alone
the gift of **UNknown** Eve of clone
to be sewn from Adam's gift of bone
for his very own (Oy, a wishbone) (Genesis 2:18 - 23).

GOD spoke to Adam
about that **UNKnown**, forbidden tree of Knowledge of Good and
Evil, full-grown, a **Known** safety zone (Oy, a danger zone of clingstones) (Genesis 2:16).

ForeKnown (Oy, tales without a tailbone)
good or bad, the serpent **Knowingly Knew**, that
Eve's interpretation of what GOD had said was matter of fact, untrue;
UNKnowingly, through the serpent's eyes, eating the fruit to Eve's surprise, would
not be her demise (Oy, the matriarch known was not to be dethroned) (Genesis 3:1-5).

In the eyes of Eve,
outgrown, with a bigger breastbone (Oy, silicone)
ingrown, it was instinctively **Known, UNKnowingly** childbearing prone, that feeding and
eating were good for Knowledge (Oy, gotta graduATE college) (Genesis 3:6),
as GOD **Knowingly** gave to Eve
alone
the gift to be the she-bearer of the womb of life, as shown (Genesis 3:20).

In the eyes of Eve,
UNKnowingly naked ... Adam ate
fruit **UNbeKnown** (Oy, a crazy bone), full of secrets, **Known** to be sacred
(Oy, bemoan, a kidney stone) and (Oy, begroan, a gallstone) (Genesis 3:6).

In the eyes of Adam,
on his own, his behavior **Known**, (Oy, a poor retinal cone)
Eve was **UNKnowingly** blamed (Oy, a jagged jawbone) and disowned,
Eve was on her own "sticks and stones may break my bones, but
names... I married a doggone knucklebone" (Oy, a combat zone) (Genesis 3:12).

In the eyes of GOD,
Adam did not acKnowledge his **Known** misdeed
for a commandment intoned, that he had **Known**, and must atone,
(Oy, poor earphones), out of tune and out of tone, monotone, if only he had **KNOWN!**
OY, a CYCLONE of hailstones "fire and brimstones"; cause GOD has no funny bone (Genesis 3:17-19)
... **UNKnowingly** rezoned (Oy, an eroding ozone)
Adam tiller of the Garden of Eden (Oy, a tropical zone)
well Known is overthrown to till (Oy, my backbone),
the overblown soil of an overgrown windblown, grass-grown garden **UNKnown** (Oy, the grindstone):
fieldstone, sandstone, millstone, cobblestone, soapstone, drystone, ironstone, and limestone are RESEWN
with firestone and paving stone into capstone, cornerstone, copestone, curbstone, foundation stone, and brownstone,
OY, Adam's aching shoulder bone, hipbone, thighbone, knee bone, anklebone, chinbone, and shinbone (Oy, muscle tone)
(Genesis 3:23).

GOD gave Eve
of her very own (Oy, Adam was outshone) the **Known** joyful gift of
a pubic bone, for **UNKnown** painful childbirth, holding her own, groan, a milestone (Oy, phenobarbitone)
(Genesis 3:16).

Adam and Eve gave to Each Other (Oy, hormones of progesterone and testosterone)
the **Known** cheekbone (Oy, seductive eau de cologne, and a gramophone playing a saxophone) of
homegrown unforbidden immense sexual passion unchaperoned (OY, OY, ALONE) and
UNforeKnowingly, unforeseen orgasmic pleasures unforetold OY, OY, PHERO-MOANS (Genesis 4:1).
Enthroned, Adam gave Eve a **well Known** precious stone, a glistening gemstone, not made of
UNknown birthstone, cinnamon stone, moonstone, toadstone or rhinestone (Oy, a touchstone).

Adam and Eve gave GOD
Future Generations of **KNOWN** (Oy, a microphone) and **WELL KNOWN** (Oy, a megaphone) and
UNKnown, no speakerphone or dialtone on the telephone or cellphone (Oy, postponed, Oy, Oy, Oy Vai Iz Mir!
"DUST to dust" gifts, a loan; and a gravestone [Oy, a tombstone of headstone or footstone?]
of **KNOWING** -a stepping stone- (Oy, a rosetta stone or philosophers' stone) and
unKnowing -on their own- (Oy, accident prone)
(Genesis 5:1).

To Be Continued ...

I gave Eve, the first woman in the Bible a **VOICE**, and liberated her from **5000** years of **MISOGYNY**.
Someone Had To Do It!

Sharon Esther Lampert
Sexiest Creative Genius in Human History
8th Prophetess of Israel: 22 Commandments
© All Rights Reserved.

www.PoetryJewels.com
Diamonds, Emeralds, Sapphires, Rubies, and Pearls

THE SOLE INTENTION OF MY POETRY IS TO ADD LIGHT TO YOUR SOUL

POETRY WORLD RECORD "Through the Eyes of Eve"
120 Words of Rhyme from One Family of Rhyme

Stanza One: Gift of Eve
1. foreshown
2. alone
3. unknown
4. clone
5. sewn
6. bone
7. own (kabbalistic significance)
8. wishbone (kabbalistic significance)

Stanza Two: Forbidden Fruit
9. full grown
10. known (kabbalistic significance)
11. safety zone
12. danger zone
13. clingstones

Stanza Three: Eve's Gift
14. foreknown
15. tailbone
another rhyme: knew, untrue
another rhyme: eyes, surprise, demise
16. dethroned

Stanza Four: Serpent
17. outgrown
18. breastbone (kabbalistic significance)
19. silicone
20. ingrown
21. prone
another rhyme: eating, feeding
another rhyme: knowledge, college
22. shown (kabbalistic significance)

Stanza Five: Adam Eats Fruit
another rhyme: naked, sacred
23. unbeknown
24. crazybone
25. bemoan
26. kidney stone
27. begroan
28. gallstone

Stanza Six: Adam Blames Eve
29. retinal cone
30. jawbone
31. disown
32. sticks and stones may break my bones
33. doggone (kabbalistic significance)
34. knucklebone
35. combat zone

Stanza Seven: The Exile
36. intoned
37. atone
38. earphone
39. tone
40. monotone (kabbalistic significance)
41. cyclone
42. hailstone
43. brimstone
44. funny bone
45. rezoned
46. ozone
47. tropical zone
48. well known
49. overthrown
50. backbone
51. overblown
52. overgrown
53. windblown
54. grass-grown
55. grindstone
56. fieldstone
57. sandstone
58. millstone
59. cobblestone
60. soapstone
61. drystone
62. ironstone
63. limestone
64. resewn
65. firestone
66. paving stone
67. capstone
68. cornerstone
69. copestone
70. curbstone
71. foundation stone
72. brownstone
73. shoulder bone
74. hipbone
75. thighbone
76. knee bone
77. anklebone
78. chinbone
79. shinbone
80. muscle tone

**Stanza Eight:
Eve's Gift of Childbirth**
81. outshone
82. pubic bone
83. groan
84. milestone
85. phenobarbitone

**Stanza Nine:
Adam and Eve's Gift (SEX)**
86. hormone
87. progesterone
88. testosterone
89. cheekbone
90. eau de cologne
91. gramophone
92. saxaphone
93. homegrown
94. unchaperoned
95. phero-moans
96. enthroned
97. precious stone
98. gemstone
99. birthstone
100. cinnamon stone
101. moonstone
102. toadstone
103. rhinestone
104. touchstone

**Stanza Ten:
Future Generations**
105. microphone
106. megaphone
107. speakerphone
108. dialtone
109. cellphone
110. telephone
111. postpone
112. loan
113. gravestone
114. tombstone
115. headstone
116. footstone
117. stepping stone
118. rosetta stone
119. philosopher' stone
120. accident prone

Philosophy Zone

Known and UnKnown

Stanza One: Adam's Gift of Eve
- **Known:** God
- Unknown: Eve

Stanza Two: Forbidden Fruit
- **Known:** Tree of Life
- Unknown: forbidden fruit

Stanza Three: Serpent
- **Known:** serpent
- Unknown: Eve

Stanza Four: God's Gift to Eve
- **Known:** God
- Unknown: childbearing

Stanza Five: Adam Eats Fruit
- **Known:** sacred secrets
- Unknown: fruit

Stanza Six: "Combat Zone"
- **Known:** Adam's behavior
- Unknown: Eve is blamed

Stanza Seven: The Exile
- Well Known: Garden of Eden
- **Known:** Commandment
- Unknown: Adam is rezoned

Stanza Eight: Eve's Gift
- **Known:** joyful children
- Unknown: painful childbirth

Stanza Nine: Adam and Eve's Gift
- **Known:** sexual passion
- Unknown: orgasmic pleasure
- Well Known: glistening gemstone
- Unknown: stones

Stanza Ten: Future Generations
- Well Known: megaphone
- **Known:** mircrophone
- Unknown: accident prone

Yiddish Translations:
Oy: interjection, denotes a negative emotion
Oy Vai Iz Mir: woe is me

Bible Zone: Dvar Torah
Princess Kadimah's Interpretation of Adam and Eve:
1. God creates the world and separates light from darkness, day from night, evening from morning, rivers from earth,sky, seasons, days and years.
2. God creates Adam and Eve, and they are living in the Garden of Eden or in **God's womb** and they are attached by **God's umbilical cord,** and God has to give birth to them (separate). When Eve eats the fruit, she has reached maturity, and it is time for God to give birth to Adam and Eve, to separate from them. Adam and Eve exit God's womb to serve God and continue the creation.

Poetry Review

"Through The Eyes of Eve"

A Poetic Classic, Deeply Philosophical, Eternally Feminine, Biblical & Modern, Melodious, Mystical, Scholarly and, Oh (Oy), So Very Humorous, **JUST DIVINE!"**
—E. Peters

---

1. Poetry segues into philosophy, comedy, and Biblical scholarship.

2. There is a universal message of **knowns** and **unknowns** for all people of all ages.

3. There is a reinterpretation of the text, the drama between Adam and Eve that finally sets Eve free from 5000 years of misogyny—Eve is now a liberated woman!

10 Poetry Reading Tips

1. Begin reading the poem to yourself silently.
2. Become familiar with the poem.
3. Read the poem by feeling and following the rhythm.
4. Take note of words needing emphasis.
5. Take note of places to pause.
6. Get to know the poem well.
7. Read the poem aloud in a natural voice.
8. Read the poem for surface meaning.
9. Reread the poem for the larger meaning of underlying ideas and depths of emotional power.
10. After reading the poem, reflect silently.

Haitian Earthquake, Port-Au-Prince, January 13, 2010
Crimes of Insanity Against Humanity

An abandoned Haitian child wanders the streets alone.
His home is an archeological ruin of collectible fragments.
His family is buried alive, entrapped and entombed in rubble.
His ancestors are unearthed and cannot rest in peace.
His dog collects and chews on the bones.
His school is decimated and classmates are presumed dead.
His church cathedral is cracked, crushed, and crumbles.
His government palace is shattered, smashed, and splinters.
His hospital is defaced, disfigured, and devastated.
His prisoners are left unscathed, and are set free to use and abuse.
His God has forsaken them, cursed them, and destroyed them.
He is immeasurably heartbroken, humiliated, and hungry.
The earth continues to shake, rattle, and roll underneath his calloused feet.

Text ten dollars to the Red Cross.
Save one body from the rubble.
Save one leg from amputation.
Save one belly from hunger.
Save one heart from pain and suffering.
Save one voice to pray for forgiveness to the devil who is in the details.
Two wrongs don't make a right: Punish the sin, not the sinner.
God should be put on trial for crimes of insanity against humanity.
The earth continues to shake, rattle, and roll underneath their calloused feet.

We are all the living dead, awaiting our demise, our final destiny.
Pyrrhic victories. Time cannot heal us. Time hurts us. Time crushes us.
There is hell on earth and hell below the earth: We will never rest in peace.
Soon the rainy season will soak their tents, and soon after the hurricane season will level them.
Justice: God is put on trial, found guilty of all crimes against humanity, and declared insane.
Until then, the earth continues to shake, rattle, and roll underneath our calloused feet.

By Sharon Esther Lampert

@All Rights Reserved. Sharon Esther Lampert.

#1 Poetry Website for Student Projects

WORLD FAMOUS POEM
TSUNAMI

How many tears can the ocean hold?
What the history books don't tell you
Is that the Indian Ocean was formed
By thousands of years of tears
That flowed from the fishermen of Sumatra.
Their pain was unbearable.
Their poverty was immeasurable.
Little to eat, little to wear,
Little to learn, too little work.
They were abandoned and forsaken.
Deep within their broken silent hearts,
An echo was heard.
The little earth quaked –
As it could no longer hold their tears.

Tens of thousands of tears overflowed
Deadly waves, crashing ashore
Sweeping their pain out from under
Their tattered rugs of impoverishment –
Out onto the front pages of newspapers worldwide.
Finally, the world took notice of their tears:
They sent care packages of food, clothing, shelter, schools, and cash.
They sent care packages of compassion, mercy, tolerance, and love.
The tears of the fisherman brought new life to tens of thousands in pain.
Salty, salty, sea water, tears of the fallen.
Salty, salty, sea water, heals the wounds of grief.
What the history books don't tell you is
How many tears can a human heart hold
Before it cracks beneath the surface
From the strain and pain and swells open
And learns how to love.

Sharon Esther Lampert
Sexiest Creative Genius in Human History
© All Rights Reserved. January 29th, 2005
Todah Rabah to Karl, My Darling Muse

In memory of the victims in Indonesia, India, Sri Lanka, Thailand, Maldives, Somalia, and Myanmar. 200,000 people died.

#1 Poetry Website for Student Projects
www.WorldFamousPoems.com
The Greatest Poems Ever Written on Extraordinary World Events

The Militant Palestinian Toddler Terrorist

At my mother's breast
I learned how to thirst for the blood of Jews

Other toddlers learn how to live and love
I will learn how to hate Jews and die as a martyr

Other toddlers have parents that love them
My parents love to hate Jews

Other toddlers wear blue and pink
I wear a belt packed with explosives to kill Jews

Other toddlers love to cuddle adorable stuffed animals
I love to clench rocks to throw at Israeli soldiers

Other toddlers have a favorite blanket
I love to stomp on and burn American and Israeli flags

Other toddlers love to play games and laugh out loud
I have a toy chest filled with loud katyusha rockets that make Jews cry

Today I plan to kill Jewish mothers and fathers and tonight
We will all be together in heaven

In heaven I will know the love of a Jewish mother and father
And I will rest in peace

1989 (1 attack)
1990s
1993 (2 bombings)
1994 (5 bombings)
1995 (4 bombings)
1996 (4 bombings)
1997 (3 bombings)
1998 (2 bombings)
1999 (2 bombings)
2000s
2000 (5 bombings)
2001 (40 bombings)
2002 (47 bombings)
2003 (23 bombings)
2004 (17 bombings)
2005 (9 bombings)
2006 (3 bombings)
2007 (1 bombing)
2008 (2 bombings)
2015 (1 bombing)

@All Rights Reserved. Sharon Esther Lampert.

#1 Poetry Website for Student Projects

SEE THE WORLD THROUGH THE EYES OF A CREATIVE GENIUS

#1 Poetry Website for Teacher Lesson Plans and Student Projects
www.WorldFamousPoems.com
The Greatest Poems Ever Written on Extraordinary World Events

KADIMAH 8TH PROPHETESS ISRAEL

Wherever Israelis Go, Gardens Grow
Hanukkah & Israel's Mount Carmel Fire, December 2-6, 2010

By Prodigy Sharon Esther Lampert

For 4 of the 8 days of Hanukah,
The God of Moses did not show her face
And blow out the conflagration.

Prophet Elijah, who resides in
A cave on its slopes, did not
Offer his wise counsel.

A mighty Israeli heroine, Brigadier
General Ahuva Tomer, waged
Her last battle, and was consumed.

Just a teen sapling, Elad Riven,
Waged his first heroic battle and
Was consumed. If only his mother's
Tears could extinguish the fire in his heart.

Fires race to the treetops and create walls.
The flames are fierce, furious, and fearless.
They show no mercy for man, beast, or flower.

Dry combustible wood and strong
Winds feverishly incinerate the
Living into black soot and ash.

Billows of smoke blanket the sky, like
Crematoria of six German gas chambers:
**Kiryat Bialik, Tirat Hacarmel, Denya
Beit Oren, Usfiya, and Ein Hod.**

The oak tree's roots are buried
Deep beneath the ground,
And they will rise again.

The Aleppo pine cones eject
Their winged seeds and settle in
The soil elsewhere, to rise again.

A bus is burned beyond recognition AS
IF blown to bits by Palestinian suicide
Bombers. Dental remains of 42 **Security Forces**
Will confirm their existence and fill their coffins.
30 children have lost the love of a parent.
Is Efrat Cohen's engagement ring redeemable?

During the Holocaust, the Jews cried out,
And everyone heard, but no one listened,
And six million Jews perished. It is Hanukah,
The season of a miracle, yet unfathomable.

Five million Jewish trees have perished.
**Wherever Jews Go, Grass Grows;
Wherever Israelis Go, Gardens Grow.**
There are no mighty Jewish warriors who
Will come to her rescue with the help of the
Outstretched hand of God, to perform a miracle.
It is a national trauma. Israeli power is powerless.

So **ISRAEL** cries out to the nations of the world,
And for the outstretched hand of the God of
Gentiles, and they saturate her air space with
Their birds of steel: In 24 hours, 10 airplanes are
In the air dousing the flames. In 48 hours, 33
airplanes are in the air, dousing the flames, and
16 more are en route ready to douse the flames.

12 Gentile nations, like brothers, come out
Of the heavens, and vanquish her enemy.
Israel has real friends, who are not fellow Jews,
Living among the Gentiles, but Gentiles who
Heard her cry out in pain, in her own homeland,
And came to her aid after her first tear was shed.
This is the **MIRACLE** that occurred on Hanukah.
This Hanukah we usher in a new **AGE OF PEACE**.

1. Greece 2. Turkey 3. Netherlands 4. Belgium 5. Germany 6. Finland 7. Norway 8. Russia 9. Switzerland 10. Cyprus 11. United Kingdom 12. USA EVERGREEN 747 SUPERTANKER

@All Rights Reserved. Sharon Esther Lampert.

POETRY IS AN ESSENTIAL SERVICE
www.PoetryEssentialService.com

Poetry Is Contagious!
Spread the Word...
Stay Home Write Verse
Save Lives and Literature!

Sharon Esther Lampert
Poet, Prophet, Philosopher, Peacemaker, Prodigy
Poem: "The World We Left Behind"

#1 Poetry Website for Student Projects

POETRY IS AN ESSENTIAL SERVICE

www.WorldFamousPoems.com
The Greatest Poems Ever Written on Extraordinary World Events

Coronavirus: The World We Left Behind

PoetryEssentialService.com

(1) I had a very bad dream that haunted me all day. I woke up to a new world order. A virus had taken over the world, and declared itself the supreme leader. **Day Is Night, Night Is Day**

(2) I am running out of breath as I breathe in the virus. I feel the muscle aches, my body is chilled to the bone. I can't stand up, I lie down. The lethargy is debilitating. I remember the face of the man who sneezed in front of me on the New Year's Eve boat ride. I could pick him out in a lineup. **Day Is Night, Night Is Day**

Note:
Jan 1 2020 COVID19

June 2020 Anti-Body Test

(3) My soul speaks a final prayer as my body launches a final attack. Tissues catch bloody sputum. Antibodies rise up to destroy COVID19. A month of armed resistance with acidic gallons of vitamin C of fresh lemons. **PURmist Steam Inhaler** liberates my body, mind, and soul. **I WON!** **Day Is Night, Night Is Day**

NOTES:
God's Wrath and Biblical Plagues:
1. Water to Blood: Ex. 7:14–24
2. Frogs: Ex. 7:25–8:15
3. Lice or gnats: Ex. 8:16-19
4. Wild animals or flies: Ex. 8:20-32
5. Pestilence of livestock: Ex. 9:1–7
6. Boils: Ex. 9:8–12
7. Thunderstorm hail & fire: Ex. 9:13–35
8. Locusts: Ex. 10:1–20
9. Darkness for three days: Ex. 10:21–29
10. Death of firstborn: Ex. 11:1–12:36

CDC Plagues 2020
- Tuberculosis, Bacteria
- Malaria, Parasite
- Measles, Virus
- HIV, Virus
- Polio, Virus
- Yellow Fever, Virus
- Tropical Diseases, Bacteria

NEW YORK CITY 2020
- April 8, 2020: #799 Dead
- Total Dead: #32,000
- July 13, 2020: **No Deaths!**
- N.Y. Governor Cuomo **Flattens Curve!**

(4) It is the first night of Passover **GOD'S WRATH:** Ten Biblical plagues pass over. It is another night of a **PANDEMIC**. One virus is passing over, striking all of us, yet killing the weakest among us. **#STAYHOME** **Global Catastrophic Trauma!** This Is why **God** Is not an **Essential Service!** The Deliverers: Moses and the Ten Commandments; and Dr. Fauci, and the Ten CDC Guidelines. **THE EXODUS: PASS THE MATZAH!** Offices! Schools! Stadiums! Restaurants!

(5) Civil rights are nullified: Mitigation is enforced. We are masked and muzzled. When I breathe into my mask, My glasses fog. I can't see! I can't talk! I can't sing! I can't smile! No selfies! We shelter in place together, but die **Alone** in the Emergency Room. **Day Is Night, Night Is Day**

(6) Game On: Germ Warfare U.S.A. vs. COVID19
UNFAIR ADVANTAGES:
- Enemy Is an Invisible Mutating Monster
- Murderers Are Microbes Not Missiles!
- Viscious Cycle of Victim and Victimizer! Patricide, Matricide, Femicide, and Fraticide!
- We Murder Loved Ones—Not Enemies!

(7) **TOO LITTLE TOO LATE!** Bill Gates Sounded the Alarm! (YT, 2015)
Trump Speaks **TRUTH** to Woodward: **"This Is Deadly Stuff!"** (Jan. 28, 2020)
Trump Speaks **LIES** to American Public: **"This Is Just a Flu!"** (Functional Psychotic)
HOPELESS: President Trump's USA **PANDUMBIC** is the World's Worst Crisis.
HOPE: N.Y. Governor Andrew Cuomo **FLATTENS THE CURVE!** (July 13, 2020)

(8) **"THE TRUMP VIRUS"** The White House Flag is Lowered to Half Staff.
USA Fatalities: One Million Americans (2022) (4% of World, 20% of Cases)
Unmasked Anti-Vaxers Rejoice, **"God Will Protect Me!"** (Bag Em-Tag Em!)
Divine Intervention: **"God Helps Those Who Help Themselves!"**
A Silver Lining: 6-feet apart sounds like a **WORLD PEACE PLAN!**

(9) We **ZOOM** into our future. Halfsies: neckties & pajamas Children dare not go out and play. Lovers dare not meet, eat, and make love. We can only **DAYDREAM** of **THE WORLD WE LEFT BEHIND**

Sharon Esther's brain conceptualizes **BIG IDEAS** using one letter of alphabet:
- **CUPID:** Languages of Love —Written in Letter **C**
- **TEMPORARY INSANITY** —Written in Letter **S**
- **SECRET SAUCE** —Written in Letter **P**

NYU honored Sharon Esther with an award for "Multi-Interdisciplinary Studies" (on YouTube)

By Sharon Esther Lampert
www.SharonEstherLampert.com
FANS@sharonestherlampert.com
Prodigy: 10 Esoteric Laws of GENIUS
Prophet: 22 Universal Moral Compass
Philosopher: GOD TALKS TO ME: A Working Definition of God
Poet: World Famous Poems
Peacemaker: World Peace Equation
Paladin: SMARTGRADES BRAIN POWER REVOLUTION
Pin-Up: Swimsuit Calendar
Phoenix: Covid19 Antibody Superhero

LIFESAVER!
PURmist
Classic Steam Inhaler

EPIC POEM
Spiraling Downward Upward We Stand United
911 World Trade Center Tragedy

By Sharon Esther Lampert

Note: The first part of every verse spirals downward and the last part of every verse spirals upward

(1) Maniacal terrorists strike at the big apple of America's eye. Famed majestic landmarks, the Twin Towers crumble, imploding into billions of bits of molten steel, jagged glass, seared human flesh, and flailing broken bones. Escaping spiked and surging fire balls, staff vaulted through windows. A canine-toothed wing of the Pentagon is broken in the aftermath of the devastation: a massive death toll of innocents remains lodged, buried alive, fifty feet under, feeling the cold-bloodied hard rubble, a steely glint of hope, five warm-blooded survivors are unearthed. Every save a divine miracle. Subways evacuate. **First-aid crews** take to the streets and man the flaming towers. Spiraling Downward, Upward We Stand United.

(2) Flattened, the first company of New York City's finest fire fighters, police, and first-aid crews CRASH and BURN inside the cascading avalanche of steel daggers. The 110-story Twin Towers are brought to their saber knees and then to their foiled ankles. Grieving, a 47-story sister building 7, collapses in distress into ragged ruins. Billowing, nearby brother buildings in the zone remain ablaze. WTC mass exodus: pyre and plumes of smoke hover, flying concrete shards and soot, repugnant jet fuel, raining dust and debris, thousands of frightful fleeing bystanders are entombed. Fatalities, makeshift morgues ferry the sacrificial corpses to New Jersey. The Pile, 1.2 billion tons of scorched scraps are hauled to The Hill of Fresh Kills Landfill. DNA matches: a gruesome, grueling, and grisly task, steam still rising, pickaxes poke for parts. Dogs sniff and succor. Ground Zero: dug-up remains are draped with the U.S.A. flag, saluted, and reburied. Every find a divine miracle. FDNY Firefighters, Jack Tipping finds his fallen son, John Jr. Tipping. A carnivorous crater, vestiges of an office complex, in the dangerous pit of dignified souls, hard hat archaeologists dig among the ruins: 13 bodies, 10 fearless firemen and 3 fearful civilians are found 30 feet below ground. High-flying stars and stripes fly low at half staff. **Busy bees swarming,** scalpeled surgeons, bedpan nurses, and selfless volunteers man the hospitals. Boiling vigorously, New Yorkers from every mosaic melting hot-pot take to the streets and wait for hours to donate their warm vital blood.

Spiraling Downward, Upward We Stand United

(3) Slamming, ramming into Grade A U.S. Steel,
four American jumbo jets are commandeered:
flight crews are maced; by razor blade box cutters,
pilots are knifed, passengers use their cell phones:
"I Love You" are their final words. Diabolical,
suicide bombers -- American men, women, and
children transfigured into four human missiles:
8:45 a.m.:Flight 11, Boeing 767, Boston to L.A.,
81 Americans, eleven crew members, CRASH
and BURN, into the north tower, N.Y.C.
9:03 a.m.:Flight 175, Boeing 767, Boston to L.A.,
56 Americans, nine crew members, CRASH
and BURN, into the south tower, N.Y.C.
9:45 a.m.:Flight 77, Boeing 757, Washington to L.A.,
58 Americans, six crew members, CRASH
and BURN, into the Pentagon, in D.C.
10:00 a.m.:Flight 93, Boeing 757, N.J. to San Francisco,
38 Americans, seven crew members, CRASH
and BURN, into an empty field, in PA, by unsung heroes:"Let's Roll!"
Federal aviation officials ground flights: 4000 planes take a nose-dive at the nearest airport. Soaring sky high, safe and sound, squawking seagulls with whimpering wings remain in flight and brave the fight. Zippered up, bridges, tunnels, and highways lock gates. Fiercely, five warships, frigate ships, and aiming bull's-eye, guided missile destroyers man the N.Y. coast: Two aircraft carriers: USS George Washington and USS John F. Kennedy man the N.Y. skies. Operation Noble Eagle: combat air patrol to shoot-em-up and shoot-em-down. In steely determination, it is business, but not business as usual.

Spiraling Downward, Upward We Stand United

(4) It is more than a terrorist attack -

It is an act of war! It is a national tragedy!

The free and democratic world is attacked:

White House evacuates.

United Nations evacuates.

Treasury evacuates.

State Department evacuates.

Justice Department evacuates.

World Bank evacuates.

All Federal office buildings evacuate.

Israel evacuates all diplomatic missions - 12 months of merciless jihad: soulless suicide bombers maim, mutilate, and murder Jews.

All N.Y. State government offices evacuate.

New York's primary elections are postponed.

Trading is suspended: The American Stock Exchange, Nasdaq, and New York Stock Exchange. 110 stories, Chicago's Sears Tower evacuates. Homeless, a frozen zone, 20,000 N.Y.C. residents are displaced. Chartering a Saudi jet, on a one way ticket to Mecca, 11 Bostonian bin Ladens evacuate.

Slumbering, F.B.I., C.I.A., I.N.S., and N.S.A. agents rouse. It is the first war of the 21st century! No-man's land, hermetically sealed, the President of the U.S.A. is whisked away. Blinding black smoke and clouds raining ash, heroic, Lady Liberty stands tall in the New York Harbor.

Spiraling Downward, Upward We Stand United

(5) Mayor Rudolph W. Giuliani addresses New York:

"Deaths are more than any of us can bear."

Senator Hillary D. Rodham Clinton addresses New York:

"We will not be cowed by evil, despicable acts of terror."

President George W. Bush addresses the nation:

"These acts shattered steel but they

cannot dent the steel of American resolve."

"We will make no distinction between the terrorists

who committed these acts and those who harbored them."

"Whether we bring our enemies to justice, or bring

justice to our enemies, justice will be done."

Nefarious doings, suspect numero uno is "The Evil One," cannibal Saudi militant

Osama bin Laden and his vile circus of vicious cavemen. Virulent videos made visible,

rallying all Muslims with venom and vitriol: "God Willing, America's end is near…

" UPWARD UNITED WE STAND: OPERATION INFINITE JUSTICE: SEEK

AND DESTROY AL QAEDA. OPERATION

ENDURING FREEDOM: target cells, villainous metastasizing cancers.

Flight 93 terrorist manhunt: Who is the 20th hijacker? Ramzi Omar or Moussaoui(?)

Americans man their maps and ask: Where the HELL (?) is Afghanistan(?)

WW III: Worldwide Coalition Bombers vs. Terror-Bender Troglodytes.

Oct 7th: Billion dollar bombs drop. Tora Bora caves are wiped off the map:

"Osama, Peek-a-Boo, Where Are You?" Taliban women see the light of day,

Taliban men will never again see the light of day. Anthrax: Biological,

nuclear, and radiological weapons. Inhalation. Evacuation. Annihilation.

"Our nation, in our fight against terrorism, will uphold the doctrine of either you're with us or against us." "And the rockets' red glare, the bombs bursting in air"

"America was targeted for attack because we're the brightest beacon for freedom and opportunity in the world. And no one will keep that light from shining." "God Bless America, land that I love. Stand beside her, and guide her…"

Spiraling Downward, Upward We Stand United.

(6) Heaven sent, where 70 virgins await each Islamic martyr on a homicidal-suicidal mission, 19 corrosive terrorists pulverize into an Arabian desert sand storm: desolate and deserted; no bad guys; no car chase; no planes; no black boxes, no survivors, no witnesses, no testimonies, no revenge to seek; no justice to exact; no war to win; and no Hollywood movie. Arise: Awake. New world order and Office of Homeland Security: cockpit dead bolts, armed pilots and martial art stewardesses, no curb side check-in and Arab profiling strip searches. An inferno, charred bodies incinerate into ashes, few funerals, many memorial tributes, urns of WTC dirt comfort. Cremated. Sobbing. Closure. Weeping widows, wailing orphans, donations flood the Red Cross. International terrorism: a worldwide menace. Terrorists: a worldwide monstrosity. **Arise: Reborn.** One true empyrean:a phoenix, names of loved ones are inscribed on the walls of the observation deck, sacred ground, a shrine, the hatched angels hover, protecting the Twin Towers rebuilt. Lighting a blowtorch, ironworkers, engineers, teamsters, laborers, and dock builders take turns... Last steel column of 2WTC, 58 tons, no. 1,001B, is cut down at 8:17 p.m. Heartbroken, resting in peace, archangel-chief architect Minoru Yamasaki said, "A beautiful solution of form and silhouette. " WorldWISE: democracy, liberty, freedom, love, prosperity, goodness, security, and peace. We Shall Overcome.

Spiraling Downward, Upward We Stand United.

(7) **A cataclysmic collision course between good and evil; angels aflight and devils afoot.** "Thou Shalt Not Murder," the first set of twin tablets of the Ten Commandments crumble into rubble, and are reengraved: Operation Infinite Circle. Singed aftershocks: fear, disbelief, terror, rage, grief, depression, revenge, numbness, and nightmares... and 2,990 children are without parents. Twin Tower totals: 90,000 tourists a day, 50,000 employed; 25,000 rescued; 35,000 in subway evacuated; and two-thirds empty airplanes. 8,700 casualties, each story a miracle: a raging fire ball, 82% of her body burned, Lauren Manning lives. Innocents: Fatalities from 92 nations, 343 firefighters, 265 airplane passengers, 184 at the Pentagon, and 25, 0000 people work at the Pentagon. Mournfully, 2,977 people are consumed. **Outstretched, GOD's hand of mercy, love, compassion, and nerves of steel, vanquished the evil incarnate, GOD WILLING.**

Spiraling Downward, Upward We Stand United.

By Sharon Esther Lampert

FAN MAIL
FANS@SharonEstherLampert.com

Dear Sharon,
I read your poem, "Spiraling Downward, Upward We Stand United" and found it to be interesting. **You might be the next T. S.† Eliot or Robert Frost!** Your web site is terrific and definitely stimulated my interest.
Sincerely,
—Dan

Thank you very much for sending along your poem. You've done a splendid job of caturing the moment. of course, part of the power of poetry lies in compression selecting a few details to stand for the whole experience. In this area, you have done a fine job. **Walt Whitman would be proud of you.**
Best Wishes,
—Angus Kress Gillespie

Dear Sharon,
Your expanded edition of "Twin Towers" ought to find its way into the history books for the younger generation.
Certainly this would impart a close-up feeling of what it was like.
Sincerely,
—Rachel

Hi Sharon,
It was very nice chatting with you Friday at Barnes and Noble about the dynamics of human relations etc. and then taking a look at all your web sites and your poetry site--wow, and certainly awesome!
Your WTC poem was an Opus Magnus on that event!
Regards,
—John

BE HARD
ON A WOMAN ONLY WHEN MAKING LOVE TO HER

—Philosopher Queen Sharon Esther Lampert

FASTER
Than Any Boy Anywhere Anytime Any Age

—Prodigy Sharon Esther Lampert

MINUS ZERO WOMAN

A WOMAN IS RAISED TO BELIEVE THAT WITHOUT A MAN SHE IS NOTHING ONLY TO FIND OUT THAT WITH A MAN SHE BECOMES LESS THAN NOTHING.

—Poet Sharon Esther Lampert

@All Rights Reserved. Sharon Esther Lampert.

#1 Poetry Website for Student Projects

SEE THE WORLD THROUGH THE EYES OF A CREATIVE GENIUS
STOP CAMPUS RAPE

Studs, Sluts, Saints, Sacrificial Lambs, Survivors, Suicide, Semen, Scandal, and Stigmata

By Prodigy Sharon Esther Lampert, October 29, 2015 (Final: Oct 24, 2016)

It is the first week of school
The class president invites her to a party

He plys me with alcohol (and drugzzzzz)
I don't even know his last name

He walks me home
I don't even remember his first name

I fall asleep in my bed
He Rapes me

I wake up with him on top of me:
Flight, fight or freeze?
I hope he is wearing a condom?
I hope I'm not pregnant?
I hope I don't have a sexually transmitted
disease? I hope I'm not labeled, "SLUT"?

STIGMATA: I cry RAPE kit
He cries foul: consensual sex

I scored a knockout punch
He scored a touch down

STUD: He brags to buddies of sexual conquest
I bawl to outraged parents who file a lawsuit

Boys post list of sexual conquests on wall: "SLUTS"
Girls carry Rape mattresses across campus (IVY: CU)

DNA speaks truth to power, BUT not in my case
Police don't prosecute HE SAID, SHE SAID

He won a Heisman Trophy; "CAN DO NO WRONG"
She's a LIAR: She wants a boyfriend not a booty call

Obama's Administration Cri De Coeur: 1 Is 2 Many
SACRIFICIAL LAMB: "Melia Obama Beer-Pong Incident"
R USA Secret Service fast asleep? (IVY: Brown U, 2015)

Lady Gaga belts out, "Til It Happens to U" (Raped at 19)
Oscar nominated co-writer Diane Warren molested at 12

RAPE: Usually someone U know: father, relative, teacher,
Neighbor, doctor, boss, professor, date, fiance, husband,
Compatriot (75%); or pervert hiding in bushes (25%).

RAPE: NO CONSENT (its that simple)
It's no use crying over spilled milk or SEMEN...

Every Woman Has a Story! Find Your Voice! Every Story Counts!

2015 ITS ON US.ORG
2013 VAWA: Violence Against Women Reauthorization Act
MISOGYNY: HATRED OF WOMEN (its that simple)

Colleges file FALSE reports: No campus RAPES and MURDER!
STIGMATA: It hurts their reputation and bottom line: $$$$$

SACRIFICIAL LAMB: R.I.P. Laura Dickinson (EMU 2006)
Settlement: 2.5 Million (Violations: Title IX and Clery Act)

Colleges host fraternity parties who DRINK, DRUG & GANG RAPE
Frat alumni donate millions: $$$$$ (University APES RAPE boys too!)

Yale University Zeta Psi & Delta Kappa Epsilon fraternity chants:
"We Love Yale SLUTS" and "No Means Yes! Yes Means Anal!" (YouTube video)

SACRIFICIAL LAMB Phi Kappa Psi: Valedictorian Liz Seccuro (UVA 1984)
GANG RAPE SURVIVOR: 22 years later, Rapist Beebe confesses: "Crash Into Me" (book)

THE HUNTING GROUND Rape victims become activists: "No Jane Doe!"
129 colleges across nation under investigation: "RAPE CULTURE"

Victim: Nude, bruised and bloodied; Erica Kinsman stands up and speaks out!
Victorious: Florida State University pays Erica Kinsman $950,000.00

St. Paul's Preparatory School: One STUD muffin is arrested, BOO HOO!
Owen Labrie's SACRIFICIAL LAMB Chessy Prout is under age, but stood up (5 %)

The "Senior Salute" is a high school tradition. Labrie explains,
"Welcome to an eight week exercise in debauchery, a probing
Exploration of the innermost meanings of the word sleazebag."

Under oath, Owen Labrie feigns, "Divine Inspiration" BUT two roommates
Out him, "Divine Intervention." SAINTS: H. Kremer & A. Thomson

Masquerade: Labrie crosses himself before Judge Smukler reads ruling
STIGMATA: ETERNAL DAMNATION as sex offender. The STUD cries.

Ironically, Labrie lost his 4-year full scholarship to Harvard Divinity School
All is not lost: Preach the word of CHRIST to fellow convicts- 5 STIGMATAS

(C.P) SHE SAID: "No one believes me. I was Raped. I'm SUICIDAL."
(O.L) HE SAID: "No one believes me. I'm going to jail. I'm SUICIDAL."

Labrie's 119 vulgar Facebook messages are noxious fumes that teach
St. Paul's STUD muffins (14-17) how to pork, bone, and slay women

THE HOLY TRINITY: LABRIE plans, GOD laughs, and DEVIL takes revenge;
When Labrie is porked, boned, and slayed in jail: Karmic Justice

ICON Bill Cosby: "MONSTER: 50 Allegations Drugged Sexual Assault"
The LEGEND: Cancelled, Revoked, Terminated, Arrested: Poetic Justice

RICH WHITE TRASH: President Donald Trump: "When you're a star, they let
you do it! Grab Them By The PUSSY" 12 Accusors✚: Gloria Allred Justice

Children Are Taught: "Don't Take Candy from Strangers"
WAKE UP WOMEN: "Don't Take Alcohol from Anyone"

@All Rights Reserved. Sharon Esther Lampert.

FAN MAIL
FANS@SharonEstherLampert.com

A Letter from Anne Peyton Bryant
She was One of the Women Attacked in Central Park

Dearest Sharon,

Your words so richly express the disenchantment that this horrifying experience has left upon me. The "concentric circles" you speak of nearly squeazed the life out of me, though I was unaware that these circles even existed until I was violently thrust into the center.

I recall the first time I read your poem. Frayed at the edges and ready to give in, your perspective on this tragedy served as a vital source of empowerment when I truly needed it the most. Thank you.

I hope that it continues to serve as a reminder to women who read it that fighting back is the only course of action that will effect a change in our culture --the participants in each circle must take responsibility for their contribution to this tragedy, which is now a wound on my soul that I fear I will never be able to completely heal.

Thank you so much!
—Anne Peyton Bryant

AWARD FOR STANDING UP & STANDING TALL
NOW selected Anne Peyton Bryant as a receipient of the Susan B. Anthony Award to be presented on Feb 20, 2001.

Anne Peyton Bryant

#1 Published Most Poem on the Internet

THE GREATEST POEM EVER WRITTEN ON
Central Park, N.Y.C., Sunday, June 11th, 2000, 11:30 a.m.-6:30 p.m.

Water Fight, Flight, and Tears

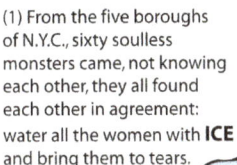

(1) From the five boroughs of N.Y.C., sixty soulless monsters came, not knowing each other, they all found each other in agreement: water all the women with **ICE** and bring them to tears.

(2) Disarmed, each woman, -fifty and counting, and countless others - is disrobed, robbed, sexually pawed, and clawed. Concentric circles form around a sole woman; a first circle of raging participants; a second circle of cheering and jeering spectators; and a third circle of indifferent police; 4500 police on duty; 900 in the park; eight calls to 911.

(3) Videotapes abound: Sexual Abuse and Violence Against Women. Madams, did it or did it not happen in our park; in the heart of the Big Apple? Men are everywhere but no real men are anywhere to be found: Too afraid: IMPOTENT are our men of the possible knife wielding soulless monsters attacking. There are no **HEROES** marching in this Puerto Rican Day Parade on **WOMEN: NADA**

(4) In childhood my father gave me an emergency whistle. Senselessly murdered, crossing Central Park, with the sun at her side, the tragedy of Joan, the beloved daughter of our distinguished Cantor, Jacob Singer, of my synagogue, sent chills down the spines and tears down the cheeks of the choking congregants, whose heart-felt ears heard the horrific news that severed their throats. On that Sabbath prayers went unheard and unanswered. An **ICEBERG:** compassion, mercy, and justice did not exist in that space in that place in the park. A sign must be posted. Where does the **EVIL** come from? Why does cold-blooded, soulless Cain have the wrong right of way to destroy the body and soul of Abel? And why is Abel unable to protect himself from his own demise?

(5) As a young adult, a canister of mace hung from the belt loop of a pant pocket or from my keychain; who knows who lurks behind unopened doors, and the upper east side rapist is still at large and nightly, he is on the prowl. Flyers of his mug hang in every doorway. At 6 a.m., I jog around the placid Central Park Reservoir, not knowing whether I am getting more fit and healthy or am I going to have myself killed.

(6) As an adult, in full bloom, it is time, says this breast bearing woman, to bear arms. Nothing less than a gun will protect my sacred soul from the soulless monsters who have no fear of daylight or police and no shame of ganging up on women, children, or the elderly. This remedy places the victimhood on the victimizers, as they are now the victims of their victimization. **JUSTICE WILL BE SERVED COLD.**

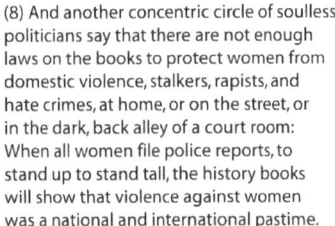

(7) Provoked, even a dog would bite off the hand or chew up the leg of one of these soulless monsters and remain on the right side of the law. Quick on a trigger, a cat would extend its sharpened claws, engraving blood lit scars into each and every face. Defenseless, women do not strike back, unable to poke out the eyes or kick in the groins of any of these soulless monsters.

(8) And another concentric circle of soulless politicians say that there are not enough laws on the books to protect women from domestic violence, stalkers, rapists, and hate crimes, at home, or on the street, or in the dark, back alley of a court room: When all women file police reports, to stand up to stand tall, the history books will show that violence against women was a national and international pastime.

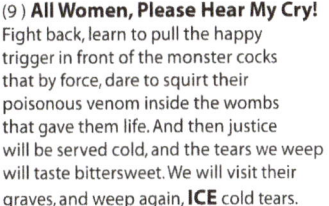

(9) **All Women, Please Hear My Cry!** Fight back, learn to pull the happy trigger in front of the monster cocks that by force, dare to squirt their poisonous venom inside the wombs that gave them life. And then justice will be served cold, and the tears we weep will taste bittersweet. We will visit their graves, and weep again, **ICE** cold tears.

"The Sole Intention of My Poetry is to Add LIGHT to Your Soul"
Having handed out this poem to park police and running mates who jog around Central Park, this poem has already inspired women to open up their hearts to me and share with me horrific assaults that they have survived at the hand of violent men who prey on women; and has empowered these same women to find the courage to file their belated police reports. I want this poem to plant a seed in the hearts of all women to fight for their civil right to be protected in their homes and in the streets.

Sharon Esther Lampert
Sexiest Creative Genius in Human History
8th Prophetess of Israel: 22 Commandments
© All Rights Reserved.

www.PoetryJewels.com
Diamonds, Emeralds, Sapphires, Rubies, and Pearls

FAN MAIL

FANS@SharonEstherLampert.com

Re: Remarks of Henry J. Stern, the Commissioner of Central Park

City of New York Parks & Recreation
The Arsenal Central Park, New York, 10021
Henry J. Stern Commissioner
November 1st, 2000

Dear Ms. Lampert,

Thank you for sending me your poem about the Puerto Rican Day Parade. The incident that occurred that day is truly a shame. Parks and all City agencies will work to ensure that nothing like it ever takes place again. It was good of you to take the time to write.

All the best,
—Henry J. Stern

Re: The Compassionate Remarks of Captain Ed Reuss of NYCOP.com

Dear Sharon,
I read your poetry with a deep feeling of shame for the actions of members of my gender. The hurt and pain that the women who were so shamefully disgraced by the men in the mobs that heaped abuse of them can never be forgotten. When chaos and the law of the jungle takes control in the streets of our city, it is always a fearsome sight.
If I were a woman, I would react with vengeful outrage at such terrorism to other women. All men, fortunately are not uncivilized beasts that prey on the weak.

May the peace of the Lord be with you.

Best wishes,
—Ed Reuss
CaptReuss@nycop.com

FAN MAIL
FANS@SharonEstherLampert.com

THAT IS GREAT!!!! THANK YOU for sending it. Can we put that in our AWSDA Journal, **The Fisted Rose?** I think our members would love it and really appreciate it.
—Elizabeth A. Kennedy
Executive Board
AWSDA

Sharon,
Used Central Park in the Blue Review this month.
http://paulie.com/blue/test.htm
There is a link at the end of the poem to your site Payment is $5..
Please confirm your address.
—Rick Russell
Editor
Blue Review

Thanks very much for sending me the link to your website and a copy of your Central Park poem. I will add a link on my Central Park page to your Central Park poem and will let you know when posted. And also review your site later for other material that may relate to my other pages.
Thanks very much.
Best,
—Mark Siporen
Editor New Nation News

Dear Sharon,
I am remiss not have written earlier. Your poetry is both potent and prophetic. I applaud your efforts to enlighten the public's awareness of the safety issues women face every day. Thank you for the email and attending my classes.
Sincerely,
—David B. Kahn
Israeli Krav Maga

Hi, Thanks for your interest in (ism). I enjoyed reading your work, especially the poem about the Central Park incidents. that was really great.
—Anna Wilson
ism poetry editor

The Fisted Rose

The Official Newsletter Of The American Women's Self Defense Association

November 2000

What's Inside...

- Editor's Note 2
- Letters to the Editor 3
- Ask the Experts 4
- If Men Got "Thwopped" 5
- Keeping The Faith 6
- Central Park Water Fight 7
- Noteworthy News 8
- Stupid Criminal 9
- Product Review 9
- An Examination of Judaism and Women's Self Defense .. 10
- Just A Walk In The Park 11
- Joe's Corner 12
- Word Search 13
- Subscription Info 13
- Corporate Sponsors 14-15

AWSDA'S WEBSITE HAS A NEW FACE!

Visit our website at
www.awsda.org

The views expressed in The Fisted Rose are not necessarily the views of AWSDA. The editorial staff encourages a provocative discussion on women's self defense and we hope to provoke discussion amongst AWSDA members by publishing articles that reflect different insights and

---

Consulting Through Conflict: Advice for the 21st Century

By Phil Messina

Fiduciary Duty means "to put some else's interest ahead of your own."

As Strategy and Tactics Consultant for this organization, I feel it is my fiduciary duty to offer my advice to AWSDA as it plunges headlong into the new millennium.

Although AWSDA has steadfastly held on to its excellent reputation and has accomplished its fundamental and philosophical goals, I believe it has still not come near reaching its full potential. In order to achieve that, it is my belief that AWSDA must accomplish the following goals within the next few years.

AWSDA Must Become More Independent Of Modern Warrior®.

That doesn't mean that Modern Warrior® should reduce its support of AWSDA in any way. It just means that AWSDA must not be dependent on that support. The fact that AWSDA is dependent on that support makes it appear to be a subsidiary of Modern Warrior® and hurts AWSDA in its efforts to attract other long term Corporate Sponsors.

The AWSDA Board Must Be More Diversified.

Since ASWDA was created (in 1990), the majority of its Board members have been affiliated in some way with Modern Warrior®. Of course that is understandable to a certain degree because it was a group of Modern Warrior® students who made up the first AWSDA Board and through the years they have worked hard and have done a very good job. However, as a ten-year-old organization, the AWSDA Board should be more representative of the political range and geographic diversity of its members. That simply means that more members who are not affiliated with Modern Warrior® must simply run for the AWSDA Board, and members who are affiliated with Modern Warrior® must vote for the long term good of the organization rather than simply voting for someone they know.

AWSDA Members Must Actively Seek Out More Corporate Sponsors And Encourage More Vendor Booths At AWSDA Seminars.

Corporate Sponsors can gain a great deal through a relationship with AWSDA. As a ten year sponsor, I have realized the value of helping a worthy cause although many do not see AWSDA as a worthy cause. They feel safer contributing money to women who have already been victimized rather than contributing to an organization who can prevent them from being victimized. It's up to AWSDA members to educate potential sponsors as to the benefit of having the nation's top consumers (women)

CENTRAL PARK: Water Fight, Flight & Tears
Central Park, N.Y.C., Sunday June, 11th, 2000 (11:30 a.m. - 6:30 p.m.)
By Sharon Esther Lampert

(1)
From the five boroughs
of N.Y.C., sixty soulless
monsters came, not knowing
each other, they all found
each other all in agreement:
water all the women with ICE
and bring them to tears.

(2)
Disarmed, each woman,
-fifty and counting, and
countless others - is disrobed,
robbed, sexually pawed and clawed.
Concentric circles form
around a sole woman; a first
circle of raging participants;
a second circle of cheering and
jeering spectators; and a third
circle of indifferent police;
4500 police on duty; 900
in the park; eight calls to 911.

(3)
Videotapes abound: Sexual Abuse
and Violence Against Women. Madams,
did it or did it not happen in our park;
in the heart of the Big Apple?
Men are everywhere but no real
men are anywhere to be found:
Too afraid: impotent are our men of
the possible knife wielding soulless
monsters attacking. There are no heroes
marching in this Puerto Rican Day Parade
on WOMEN:NADA

(4)
In childhood, my father gave
me an emergency whistle. As a
young adult, a canister of mace
hung from the belt loop of a pant
pocket or from my keychain;
who knows who lurks behind
unopened doors, and the upper
east side rapist is still at large and
nightly, he is on the prowl. Flyers
of his mug hang in every doorway.

(5)
As an adult, in full bloom, it is time,
says this breast bearing woman to bear
arms. Nothing less than a gun will
protect my sacred soul from the soulless
monsters who have no fear of daylight
or police and no shame of ganging up
on women, children or the elderly.
This remedy places the victimhood
on the victimizers, as they are now
the victims of their victimization.
JUSTICE WILL BE SERVED COLD.

(6)
Provoked, even a dog would bite-
off the hand or chew-up the leg
of one of these soulless monsters
and remain on the right side of
the law. Quick on a trigger, a cat
would extend its sharpened claws
engraving blood lit scars into each
and every face. Defenseless, women
do not strike back, unable to poke
out the eyes or kick in the groins of
any of these soulless monsters.

(7)
And another concentric circle of soulless
politicians say that there are not enough
laws on the books to protect women from
domestic violence, stalkers, rapists and
hate crimes, at home, or on the street or
in the dark, back alley of a court room:
When all women file police reports, to
stand up to stand tall, the history books
will show that violence against women
was a national and international pastime.

(8)
All Women, Please Hear My Cry!
Fight back, learn to pull the happy
trigger in front of the monster cocks
that by force, dare to squirt their
poisonous venom inside the wombs
that gave them life. And then justice
will be served cold, and the tears we weep
will taste bittersweet. We will visit their
graves, and weep again, ICE cold tears.

"My Life is an OPENBook, to KNOWMe is to READMe"

Sharon Esther Lampert (Kadimah, The Tribal Princess of Israel)   http://www.poetryjewels.com,   email queenkadimah@hotmail.com

Having handed out this poem to park police and running mates who jog around Central Park, this poem has already inspired women to open up their hearts to me and share with me horrific assaults that they have survived at the hands of violent men who prey on women; and has empowered these same women to find the courage to file their belated police reports. I want this poem to plant a seed in the hearts of all women to fight for their civil right to be protected in their homes and in the streets. —SEL

#1 Poetry Website for Student Projects

www.WorldFamousPoems.com
The Greatest Poems Ever Written on Extraordinary World Events

Sharon Esther Lampert
8TH Prophetess of Israel
Enlightenment: 24 Commandments
THE DELIVERER

First Responder Poet
December 10 2013

"Food Is for the Body,
Education Is for the Mind,
And Poetry Is for the Soul."
Sharon Esther Lampert

Martin Luther King
Enlightenment: I Have a Dream
THE DELIVERER

A Tribute to Nelson Mandela
THE DELIVERER
An Enemy and Head of State

By Sharon Esther Lampert

A difference, can one life make.
A PhD. in Freedom Fighter.

A delicate balance, a work in progress.
A coexistence, a sharing of resources.

Might does not make right.
White skin is not a privilege.

Damned if you do, damned if you don't:
Violent coup or peaceful non-cooperation?

Deliver yourself from ignorance.
Enlightenment is a long walk to freedom.

Don't die in vain, learn from your mistakes.
The **BLAME GAME** is not a solution to a problem.

Tit for Tat: All Evil Is Justified.
Two wrongs don't make a right.

Choose democracy over fascism.
Choose integration over segregation.

Choose shareholders over domination.
Choose forgiveness over revenge.

**CAST YOUR VOTE 4 HOPE
EDUCATE: MIND, BODY, AND SPIRIT**

Choose nurture over nature: LOVE, PEACE, and UNDERSTANDING.
Choose the future over the past. BE PRESENT.

Be born in apartheid (1948-1994) and fight for EQUALITY.
EMANCIPATION: Be told you're a nobody and die a somebody special.

There are good people and there are bad people, and
THERE IS NO OTHER DIFFERENCE.
Good People:Nothing Is a Problem ... Bad People:Everything Is a Problem

Be guided by your hopes, not your fears.
See future generations: **"THE BORN FREES."**

MANDIBA
Rolihlahla
Dalibhunga
Mandela
46664

MOSES
Walk to Freedom: 40 Years
Enlightenment: Ten Commandments
THE DELIVERER

The Sole Intention of My Poetry Is to Add LIGHT to Your Soul

"For to be free is not merely to cast off one's chains, but to live in a way that respects and enhances the freedom of others." N. Mandela

#1 Poetry Website for Student Projects

SEE THE WORLD THROUGH THE EYES OF A CREATIVE GENIUS

www.WorldFamousPoems.com
The Greatest Poems Ever Written on Extraordinary World

THE DELIVERER
A Tribute to Rev. Martin Luther King
By Prodigy Sharon Esther Lampert

Sharon Esther Lampert
KADIMAH 8TH Prophetess of Israel
One Ethical Code for Seven Billion People
Enlightenment: "30 Commandments"
THE DELIVERER

7 Prophetess of ISRAEL: Sarah, Miriam, Deborah, Huldah, Hannah, Abigail, Esther

First Responder Poet
December 10, 2013 (Mandela)
December 23, 2015 (King)

"Food Is for the Body,
Education Is for the Mind,
And Poetry Is for the Soul."
Sharon Esther Lampert

A difference, can one life make
A PhD. in Freedom Fighter

A delicate balance, a work in progress
A coexistence, a sharing of resources

Might does not make right
White skin is not a privilege

Damned if you do, damned if you don't
Violent coup or peaceful non-cooperation?

Deliver yourself from **IGNORANCE**
ENLIGHTENMENT is a long walk to freedom
MOSES, MARTIN, MANDIBA

WE HAVE A DREAM

Don't die in vain, learn from your mistakes
The **BLAME GAME** is not a solution to a problem

Tit for Tat: **ALL EVIL IS JUSTIFIED**
Two wrongs don't make a right

Choose democracy over fascism
Choose integration over segregation

Choose shareholders over domination
Choose forgiveness over revenge

CAST YOUR VOTE 4 HOPE
EDUCATE: MIND, BODY, AND SPIRIT

Nelson Mandela
Enemy & Head of State
THE DELIVERER

MANDIBA
Rolihlahla Dalibhunga Mandela
Prison: 27 Years (46664)
President: 1994-1999

STATE OF ISRAEL
May 14, 1948

MOSES
Walk to Freedom: 40 Years
"LET MY PEOPLE GO"
Enlightenment: Ten Commandments
THE DELIVERER

Rev. Martin Luther King
Enlightenment: "I Have a Dream"
THE DELIVERER

Choose nurture over nature: **PEACE, LOVE, and UNDERSTANDING**
Choose a **FRESH START** over righting the wrongs of the past: **BE HERE NOW**

Be born a slave (1620-1866) and set **FREE** on December 6, 1865 by the 13th Constitutional Ammendment
Be born second class (1929-1968) and fight for **EQUALITY** (The 1964 Civil Rights Act, The 1965 Voting Act)
Be born **FREE**: 44TH President of the United States of America: Barack Hussein Obama II (2009-2017)
EMANCIPATION: Be told you're a nobody and die a somebody special

There are good people and there are bad people and; **THERE IS NO OTHER DIFFERENCE**
Good People: Nothing Is a Problem ... Bad People: Everything Is a Problem

Be guided by your hopes, not your fears. See future generations: **"THE BORN FREES"**
"Free at Last, Free at Last. Thank God Almighty, We Are Free At Last"

The Sole Intention of My Poetry Is to Add LIGHT to Your Soul — Autographed Collectible

"For to be free is not merely to cast off one's chains, but to live in a way that respects and enhances the freedom of others." Nelson Mandela

Ebenezer Baptist Church, Boca Raton, Florida

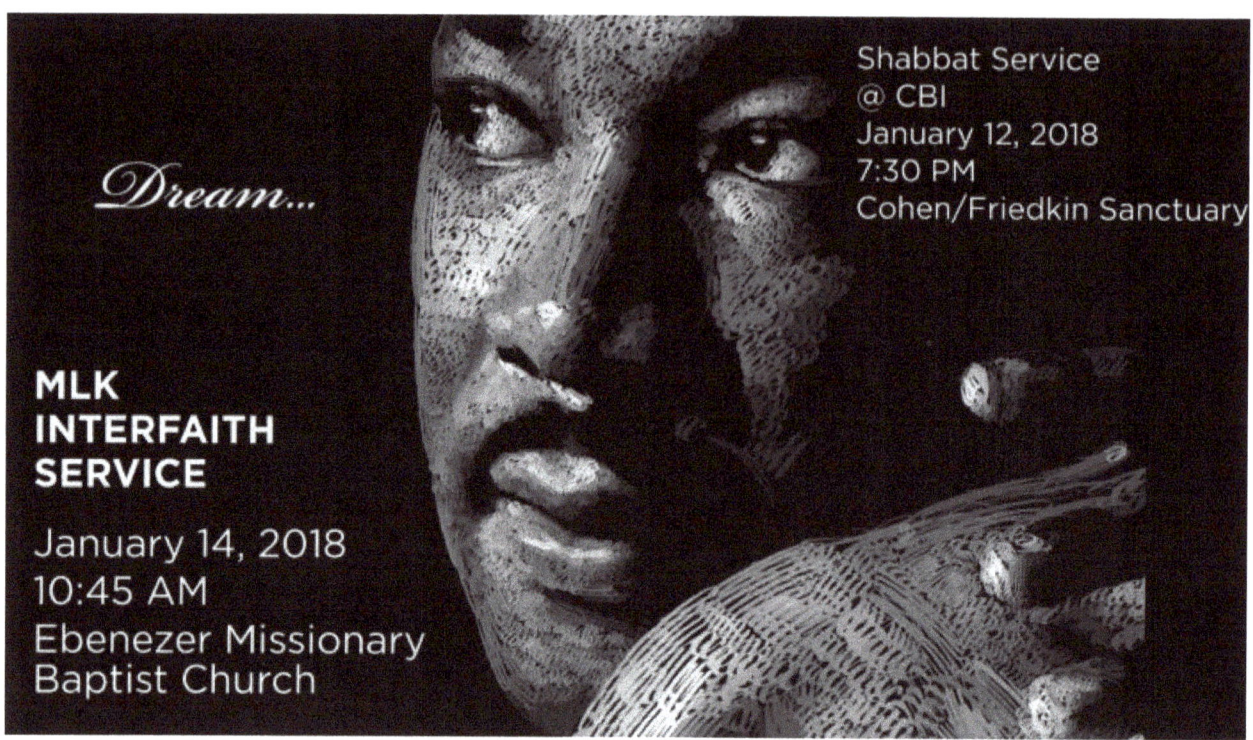

It is my great honor to read my poem, **THE DELIVERER"** in celebration of Dr. Reverand Martin Luther King Jr. on his annual birthday at the Ebenezer Baptist Church, in Boca Raton, Florida

FAN MAIL
FANS@SharonEstherLampert.com

Date: Thursday, November 19, 2009, 3:11 PM

Dear Ms. Lampert,
Hi
I am doing a poetry project for my English Honors 10th grade class and found your poem, "Simon Wiesenthal: Survivors Burden" and need the date of publication to include it in my project. I am also going to share it with my temple's confirmation class.

Thank you for getting back to me as soon as possible so I can finish my project.

Sincerely,
—Josh

So Special! A Letter from the Simon Wiesenthal Family

From: Joeri Kreisberg
Wednesday, March 29, 2006, 7:43 AM
Poem about Simon Wiesenthal

Dear Ms. Lampert,

I am in receipt of your letter to me with the poem written on my grandfather, Simon Wiesenthal.

First of all, apologies for my belated reply, which so late for various reasons, it has been quite a hectic time.

We were all very moved to receive the poem, and I made sure to distribute all copies thereof to my sister, Rachel and her husband Yossi and their three girls, Elah, Maya and Tali, to my brother Danny and his wife Orlee and their two children Liron and Shani, and of course to my wife Tamar, and our two boys David and Michael.

We very much appreciated your kind gesture, and I would like to thank you on behalf of all of us, including my parents, Paullina and Gerard Kreisberg.

All the best,
—Joeri Kreisberg
Ramat Gan 52521, Israel

#1 Poetry Website for Student Projects

THE SOLE INTENTION OF MY POETRY IS TO ADD LIGHT TO YOUR SOUL
THE GREATEST POEM EVER WRITTEN ON SIMON WIESENTHAL

Simon Wiesenthal (1908-2005)

On September 20th, 2005, Simon Wiesenthal died at the age of 96. He was born in the Ukraine. He was trained as an Architect. At age 36, he was liberated from the Mauthausen Concentration Camp. He had been imprisoned in a total of 12 concentration camps (five of which were death camps). He lost 88 relatives in the Holocaust. He married Cyla Muller, a survivor and had a daughter, Dr. Paulina Kreisberg: He has three grandchildren and seven greatgrandchildren. **He dedicated his life to tracking down, hunting, and gathering information on fugitive Nazis to bring them to justice for war crimes and crimes against humanity.**

He received many distinguished awards:
U.S. Congressional Gold Medal (1980)
French Legion of Honor (1986)
Presidential Medal of Freedom (2000)
Honorary British Knighthood (2004)
Austrian Golden Decoration of Merit (2005)

His memoirs and movies are entitled:
"I Hunted Eichmann" (1961)
"The Murderers Among Us" (1967)
"Justice, Not Vengeance: Recollections" (1989)
Academy Award-winning documentary, "Genocide"

Sharon Esther Lampert
Sexiest Creative Genius in Human History
8th Prophetess of Israel: 22 Commandments

www.PoetryJewels.com
Diamonds, Emeralds, Sapphires, Rubies, and Pearls

Todah Rabah to Karl, My Darling Muse
Written on October 6th, 2005
© All Rights Reserved

A Memorial Tribute in Poetry to Simon Wiesenthal
A Survivor's Burden

After six million Jews were silenced:
Simon speaks above a hush.
Simon speaks above a whisper.
Simon speaks above an earshot.
Simon speaks out loud above the deafening scream of EVIL.

After six million Jews were silenced:
Simon's voice shatters the ghetto walls of anti-Semitism.
Simon's voice bellows in the streets of Argentina.
Simon's voice hallows in the halls of JUSTICE.
Simon's voice harkens in the International Arena of INJUSTICE.

After six million Jews were silenced:
Simon Wiesenthal WALKS his TALK and JUSTICE is done:
Adolf Eichman is brought to JUSTICE.
Franz Stangl is brought to JUSTICE.
Franz Murer is brought to JUSTICE.
Erich Rajakowitsch is brought to JUSTICE.
Hermine Braunsteiner is brought to JUSTICE.
Karl Silberbauer is brought to JUSTICE.
Josef Schwammberger is brought to JUSTICE.
1,100 Nazi War Criminals are brought to JUSTICE.

After six million Jews were silenced:
Simon Says:
"This man is on my list as a suspected war criminal."
Simon Says:
"When history looks back I want people to know the Nazis weren't able to kill millions of people and get away with it."
Simon Says:
"If we don't do anything about evil, that will encourage future perpetrators."
Simon Says:
"My work is a warning for the murderers of tomorrow."
Simon Says:
"Survival is a privilege which entails obligations. I am forever asking myself what I can do for those who have not survived."
Simon Says:
"I have received many honors in my lifetime; when I die, these honors will die with me, but the Simon Wiesenthal Center will live on as my legacy."
Simon Says:
"My epitaph should read simply **"SURVIVOR."**
Simon Says (in the afterlife... to the six million Jews murdered in the Holocaust):
"I didn't forget you."

CHILD OF HOLOCAUST SURVIVOR'S BURDEN
I am a child of a Holocaust survivor...
The "Child of Holocaust Survivor's Burden" is to preserve the memories of the Holocaust survivor.
In this poem, I BEAR WITNESS to keep Simon Wiesenthal's message ALIVE for future generations.
I hope Simon Wiesenthal, the quintessential researcher, is proud of my ability to ferret out the facts of his life.

NOTES ON THE NAZIS:
Adolf Eichmann was a planner of Jewish extermination. Fritz Stangl was a commandant of two death camps. Franz Murer was "The Butcher of Wilno." Erich Rajakowitsch was in charge of the "death transports" in Holland. Gestapo officer Karl Silberbauer arrested Anne Frank in her Amsterdam hideout. Hermine Braunsteiner Ryan, helped process the murder of women and children at a camp in Poland and later was found living as a housewife in Queens, N.Y. SS Officer Josef Schwammberger used his German shepherd dog, Prince, to sadistically prey on Jewish inmates.

Edith Stein

Born a Jew, Became an Atheist, Converted to Catholicism Became a Nun
Gassed at Austwitz as a Jew, and Beatified a Catholic Saint

Age: 51

1. October 12, 1891
   Edith Stein was born on in Breslau, Germany (now Wroclaw, Poland)
   Born into an Orthodox Jewish family

2. 1904, Edith Stein renounced her faith and became an atheist.

3. Student at the University of Gottingen, she received her doctorate in philosophy.
   She moved to the University of Freiburg, with Edmund Husserl and became his assistant.

4. Edith into contact with Roman Catholicism and read the autobiography of the mystic St. Theresa of Avila

5. January 1, 1922:
   Edith was baptized and taught at a Dominican girls' school in Speyer (1922 - 1932).
   She translated St Thomas Aquinas' De veritate (On Truth).

6. 1932-1933
   Edith became a lecturer at the Institute for Pedagogy at Munster
   Anti-semitic legislation passed by the Nazi government, forced her to resign the post in 1933.

7. 1934:
   Edith entered the Carmelite convent at Cologne, taking the religious name Teresa Benedicta of the Cross. She completed her metaphysical work 'Endliches undewiges Sein', an attempt to synthesize the diverse philosophies of Aquinas and Husserl.

8. 1938:
   Edith was transferred to the Carmelite convent at Echt in the Netherlands because of the Nazi threat. She wrote her important treatise 'Studie uber Joannes a Cruce: Kruezeswissenschaft'. Removing her from Germany, did not ensure her safety.

9. July 26, 1942:
   Adolf Hitler ordered the arrest of all non-Aryan Roman Catholics.
   Edith and her sister was seized by the Gestapo and shipped to the concentration camp at Auschwitz. Survivors of the death camp testified that she helped all other sufferers with great compassion.

10. August 9, 1942:
    Edith was sent to the gas chamber, where she died with her sister.

11. May 1, 1987:

December, 22, 2000
Thank you for letting me know of your poem. Edith Stein was a great and important person and it is good to know that she is being heard again.
—Paul

Paul Douglas Stamm
Technology Coordinator
Divine Savior Holy Angels High School
4257 N. 100th Street
Milwaukee, WI 53222
www.dsha.k12.wi.us

#1 Poetry Website for Student Projects

THE GREATEST POEM EVER WRITTEN ON EDITH STEIN
CASTING LIGHT: Our sister, Edith Stein, of the St✡r of David; Their Sister, Teresia Benedic✞a, of the Cross

Spiritually at Unrest,
Our sister, Edith Stein recoiled into an atheist.
Her writings -forecast- a student of phenomenology; a PH.D. ascended.
Our sister, Edith Stein, of the Star of David, -cast- as an intellectual Jewess, -recast- herself
as their Sister, Teresia Benedicta of the Cross, a Roman Catholic, Carmelite Nun.

Physically at Unrest,
Once again -recast- as Edith Stein, of the Star of David, our sister, was -cast- down
into the gas chambers of Auschwitz; a yellow star was left behind.
Her Jewish identity, reconfigured into smoldering
ashes, was incontestable and unconsumable.
Life, in this world, was left behind.
All Jewish-born Catholic converts were consumed; baptism was left behind. Familiar family flaws.
Six million more Jewish souls were consumed. Silenced, eternally.
Relationships of religion, resources, and revenue were familiar family lies; baptisms by fire.
The prayers of their Sister, Teresia Benedicta, of the Cross were
-unheard- and -unanswered-

Physically and Spiritually at Unrest,
Edith Stein's Jewish identity, is -cast- back, twice,
EDITH STEIN -once- abandoned, in a concentration camp, ETERNAL DAMNATION;
EDITH STEIN -once again- forsaken, in a canonization council, DAMNED, ETERNALLY -

Once again -recast- as their Sister, Teresia Benedicta, of the Cross, our sister, Edith
Stein of the Star of David, -gassed- as one soul of the six million Jewish souls,
unable to save, secure, or salvage her own sacred soul, is -cast- up a heroic
savior, and is -recast- a saint for world-wide salvation.
Eternal life, ascended.
Their Sister, Teresia Benedicta, of the Cross, is -recast- as a Roman Catholic Martyr,
beatified in 1987, and canonized in 1998, by the Vatican, in Rome. Familiar family faith.
In between, on December 30th, 1993, the Vatican-Israel Accord was signed, and -cast- aside. Familiar family forgetfulness.
The memorial prayers, for our sister, Edith Stein, are recited on Holocaust Remembrance Day. Familiar family funeral and
folklore; Our Jewish people, eternally, living abroad in fear. Silenced.
Our sister, Edith Stein, of the Star of David, is -casting- light,
and ascending, as a Roman Catholic Saint.

Edith Stein

Spiritually and Physically at Rest,
-Cast- adrift the soul of a two year old child, Benedicta McCarthy, is -cast- down
by a Tylenol overdose, is -cast- about by seizures, and is then -cast- up : THE MIRACLE.
Familiar family fact or fiction, faith or fantasy? fallacy? HEAVEN FORBID!
Our Dr. Ronald Kleinman is their credible witness. Familiar family friend or foe?
Life, in this world, ascended.
A single soul is not consumed.

The prayers, to their Sister, Teresia Benedicta, of the Cross, are **-heard- and -answered-**

Their Sister, Teresia Benedicta, of the Cross, is **-casting- light,**
and ascending, as a Roman Catholic Saint.

Benedicta McCarthy

Physically at Unrest,
Their Eugenio Maria Giuseppe Giovanni Pacelli -cast- as a Reverend, was -recast- as Pope Pius XII:
The prayers, for the salvation of the soul of our sister, EDITH
STEIN, of the Star of David, -gassed- as one of the six million Jewish souls were
-unheard- and -unanswered-
Eternal Damnation.

Spiritually at Unrest,
Their Karol Joseph Wojtyla -cast- as a Reverend, is -recast- as Pope John Paul II:
The prayers, for the salvation of the soul of our sister, EDITH
STEIN, of the Star of David, who died a Jewess,
"Come Rosa, We Are Going For Our People,"* are
-unheard- and -unanswered-   *N.Y.T., Oct. 11, 1998
Damned, Eternally.

Sharon Esther Lampert
Sexiest Creative Genius in Human History
8th Prophetess of Israel: 22 Commandments

www.PoetryJewels.com
Diamonds, Emeralds, Sapphires, Rubies, and Pearls

THE SOLE INTENTION OF MY POETRY IS TO ADD LIGHT TO YOUR SOUL

#1 Poetry Website for Student Projects

EPIC POEM
In 5 Minutes
Learn 5000 Years of Jewish History

By Sharon Esther Lampert — In Celebration of 50TH Birthday

Many Jews Reclaimed God

By Divine Words and Divine Works, Abraham and Sarah, Isaac and Rebecca, Jacob, Leah, and Rachel conceived a holy people. Familiar family faith. In an ark, Noah was not consumed; a rainbow ascended. Adam blamed Eve, and the Garden of Eden was left behind. Joseph cast into a pit and prison, was recast as a prince of Egypt. The silver goblet ascended. Benjamin was not left behind. Familiar family forgiveness. Divine convenants of spiritual and physical dimensions were contracted with Abraham, Noah, Jacob, and Moses. Seven prophetesses ascended: Sarah, Miriam, Deborah, Hannah, Abigail, Huldah and Esther; the first beauty queen contestant. All Hebrews became physically and spiritually enslaved in Egypt; mortar descended and bricks ascended. GOD spoke to Moses and Moses once-and-once-again received The Ten Commandments. The burning bush was not consumed. Twelve tribes ascended. All of the Children of Israel received The **Ten Commandments** in the barren desert. Many Jews became spiritually liberated.

MANY JEWS HAD FOUND GOD

All Jews wanted physical deliverance from the barren desert. Many Jews found the homeland and became Israelites, a miracle. Moses was left behind. All Jews were divided into two kingdoms: Northern Kingdom of Israel in Samaria and Southern Davidic Kingdom of Judah in Judea. Some Jews remained Jews after the Assyrian exile, Babylonian exile, and destruction of the First Temple. Some Jews remained Jews after the Roman exile and destruction of the Second Temple. King Saul, King David, and King Solomon ascended. Ascending and descending, messiahs, miracles, and martyrs were left behind. All Canaanite, Philistine, Ammonite, Moabite, Midianite, Sumerian, Assyrian, Hittite, Babylonian, Persian, and Roman Empires, and ALL of their **GODS** were left behind. Dream of Zion renewed was not left behind. All Jews underwent the wear and tear of conquest, destruction, and exile.

SOME JEWS HAD FORSAKEN GOD

Exiled from their homeland, all Jews prayed for spiritual redemption from the religious oppression of the Diaspora. All Jews who remained Jews found incessant forced conversions, persecutions, and pogroms throughout Western and Eastern Europe. Thirty-four expulsions were recorded: For 2000 years, Christian hatred of the Jews consumed. Many Jews died "Al Kiddush Hashem." Thousands upon thousands of Christians fought against the enemies of Christ. Thousands upon thousands of Muslims fought against the infidels: Christians vs. Muslims (to this very day) each take turns leaving each other behind...proselytes vs. apostates. **The Greatest Lie Ever Told in the Name of GOD** descended: The death of Jesus was good for Christians and bad for Jews. For Christians: **"Jesus Died for You, So You Can Live and You Get Eternal Life."** For Jews: **"Jesus Died and You Killed Him and You Get Premature Death."** Relationships of religion, resources, and revenue were familiar family lies. Many Jews witnessed verbal slanders turned into violent physical deeds.

ALL JEWS SAW THEIR FATE IN GOD'S HANDS

All Jews and only Jews were no longer given choices: economic discrimination, social ostracism, personal humiliation, and the **"THE FINAL SOLUTION."** Familiar family lies. The yellow star descended. Jews, cast as wandering exiles, were recast for genocide. Swastikas descended. Less than one fourth of one percent of the world's population were targeted for extermination. Shaved heads and tatooed numbers burned into arms descended. Many Jews were deported to concentration camps (human flesh burning crematoria, gas chambers, and hospital rooms for scientific experimentation): Zyklon-B gas was consumed. One third of worldwide Jewry was annilated. Six million sacred Jewish souls were left behind, their physical bodies exterminated, their seeds of immortality extinguished. A few Jews committed suicide on their way to, inside of, and soon after, the ominous death camps.

SOME JEWS LOST GOD

Homebound, all Jews wanted to go home. Some Jews had families and some Jews were orphans. All Jews were the children of God. Ascending, some Jews went to Canada; a few Jews went to South Africa where the world was divided into white on black; a few Jews went to Argentina with the escaped Nazis. The Jewish Brigade of Palestine was not consumed. The slogan, **"Jews Can Fight and Jews Can Win"** ascended. In the Pope's office, blaming the Jews for **DEICIDE** was left behind. UN Resolution 3379, Zionism was Racism, was left behind. Many Jews went to America with ALL worldwide refugees (to this very day). On the Statue of Liberty, Emma Lazarus's poetry ascended. Irving Berlin's compositions, "God Bless America" and "Israel" ascended. Ascending, the sexiest woman alive, Marilyn Monroe, converted to Judaism. In Sweden, Alfred Nobel, cast as a dynamite manufacturer, was recast as the good will manufacturer of Nobel Prizes. Jewish genius ascended and was recognized: For WORLD PEACE: Alfred H. Fried (1911); ... For ECONOMICS: Paul A. Samuelson (1970); ... For CHEMISTRY: Adolph Von Baeyer (1905);... For PHYSICS: Albert Abraham Michaelson (1907);... For MEDICINE and PHYSIOLOGY: Elie Metchnikoff (1908); ... Jews hold 20% of the Nobel Prizes. Jews wrote the popular Christmas songs: White Christmas, Rudolph, The Red-Nosed Reindeer, Let it Snow, Silver Bells, and Chestnuts Roasting on the Open Fire. Ascending, worldwide, humanity as a whole benefits from these magnificent, monumental, and momentous contributions from less than one fourth of one percent of the world's population. In 50 countries, Lubavitch-Chabad emissaries were left behind and not consumed: Jewish spiritual reinvigoration ascended. Many Jews witnessed a glimmer of the glorious face of **GOD**.

SOME JEWS SAW GOD EVERYWHERE

HOME SWEET HOME: Jews from every country in the world went home: Jews from 102 countries, speaking 82 languages ascended. On May 14, 1948, the vision of Theodor Herzl ascended: First as pioneers, then as soldiers and citizens, and finally as Zionists. The national anthem, **"Hatikvah,"** ascended. The Hebrew language ascended. Falafel in pita with tehina sauce was consumed. A miracle: "The Old Israel's" GOD YHWH was not consumed in the Holocaust. Triumphant, the Israel Defense Forces ascended. All Jews, cast as sacrificial lambs, were recast as sacrificial LIONS: Arab Riots and Revolts, War of Independence, Suez Canal, Six-Day War, Yom Kippur War, Lebanon War, Iraqi Scud Missile Crisis, and Incessent Terrorism descended. The Nation of Israel reborn was reckoned with, reconciled with, and was recognized by the world. Israeli operations resettled the exiles and unsettled the enemies. In this birthplace of ancient miracles, modern miracles of medicine, science, and technology ascended. Democracy ascended. The nomads of the desert were not consumed; civilization was not an oasis. The greetings, "Shalom Aleichem" among Jews and "Salam Aleikem" among Arabs acsended: "Baruch Hashem," and "Inshallah": an imperfect PEACE is ascending in an imperfect world, birthplace of the One and Only Perfect GOD. **The tri-part unity of the Jewish people, the Torah and the Biblical Homeland set a historical precedent.** God's promise of a land flowing with milk and honey is ascending: *"Wherever Jews Go, Grass Grows; Wherever Israelis Go, Gardens Grow."* This year of 5758 is the State of Israel's 50th Anniversary. The Jewish historical past was in the Diaspora; the historical future is in Israel. Some Jews born in Israel live everywhere... on temporary leave. **Israel is the only HOMELAND these Jews will ever know!**

MANY JEWS RECLAIMED GOD

For My Love, Dr. C. Silk

My Stand-up Comedy Bits

THAT WOMAN IN RED
My Short Funnies on My Long Feelings

The Safest Woman in the World to Make Love To

I happen to be the safest woman in the world to make love to...

because all of my boyfriends were doctors, and each one of them subjected me to a complete physical before making love to me, and i always passed with flying colors...

with only one exception...

There was this 6ft 8, 220 pound dentist, who told me that he wanted to make love to me but he would never marry me... because I have too many cavities.

Most women in my shoes, with my mouth would say, "You Can't Have Me"... but I could tell that he packed a BIG DRILL, and so I let him have his way with me.

He filled all of my holes, little holes, and big holes, on the tops, and I the bottoms...I was screaming in ecstasy...

I felt completely fulfilled in the relationship...

...and I have a clean bill of health from the American Dental Association.

Sharon Esther Lampert
The Comedy of the Sexiest Creative Genius in Human History

For My Love, Dr. B. Ginsberg

Dating a Gynecologist

I'm dating a gynecologist.

On our very first date, he wants to make love to me.

I said: "Only on one condition,
Dr. Bernard Ginsberg.

Only if you throw in a FREE breast exam and a FREE pelvic exam."

He did.

It was all KOSHER.

He also threw in dinner and a Broadway show.

This was the best medical treatment I have ever received.

He was a much better lover than my regular gynecologist... "WHAM-BAM...
Two Hundred and Fifty Dollars...
Thank You, Mam!"

Sharon Esther Lampert
The Comedy of the Sexiest Creative Genius in Human History

FIRST LOVE

SEE THE WORLD THROUGH THE EYES OF A CREATIVE GENIUS

As a college freshman, I was relentlessly pursued by an Italian-Catholic boy.

He asked me out to a movie:
I told him I couldn't go because "I AM JEWISH!"
He asked me where I was from: I said, "I AM JEWISH!"
He asked me what my major was: I said, "I AM JEWISH!"
He asked me what I wanted to be when I grow up – I mean graduated!
I said, "I AM JEWISH!"

For three months, he placed love notes into my dorm-room mailbox.
I still have them.

"With love's light wings did I o'er-perch these walls, for stony limits cannot hold love out," said Romeo.

He was brilliant, a Presidential scholar.
He was gorgeous, a member of the basketball team
He came from an all-boys Catholic high school;
I came from a Solomon Schecter Day School.
He said he wanted to convert.

What did he see in me? I had a mouth full of metal braces.
He gave me a button that said, "Tin-Grin." I have that too!

Love notes and all, he became irresistible:
The last image I remember before I got very lost in the throes of ecstasy was of a wooden statue of JESUS hanging over his bed.
We were all naked.
Two of us were Jews.
Him, Me, JESUS: a Holy Trinity.
He had made me a woman.

Later, I was very miserable over the fact that I was so happy.

"I AM JEWISH...WOMAN!" Mazel Tov!

The nouveau Romeo & Juliet had met each other's parents too!

3 out of 4 parents wished them well—the 4th parent was a Jewish-Holocaust survivor.

"O happy dagger! This is thy sheath; there rust, and let me die," said Juliet.

When he grew up – I mean graduated! – he became, "A Nice-Catholic Doctor"... a Psychiatrist.

I was his first patient! — Parting is Such Sweet Sorrow, said Juliet.

"For never was a story of more woe than this of Juliet and her Romeo," said, William Shakespeare.

"Tin Grin" Sharon Esther Lampert
One of the World's Greatest Poets

For My Love, Y.J. Jacks, United Kingdom, Israeli-Englishman

THAT KISS

Fortune teller that I AM,
My crystal ball sees ALL.
Clairvoyant, the man's libido is flam**BOY**ant.
I SEE: **ANIMAL MAGNETISM.**
Inside of **THAT KISS** will be BLISS.

Taking chances with amorous glances,
He advances... Lips pouting-tongue tied:
THAT KISS: SmOOch; smOOch.
When he romances: his gait prances,
His penis lances, his generosity enhances.
VOODOO, or DOO-YOU want dinner, dear?"
His heart dances....

Magician that **HE IS**,
He has a loaded deck of cards,
And wants to be my bodyguard.
Enchantment: a bag of mesmerizing tricks,
An **ACE** up his sleeve, a **KING** or a **JACK**
Are inside of his top hat of black.
Sleight of hand, **THAT KISS** is grand.

WIZARDRY: Pressed into his bosom,
I am caught in his embraces, arms
Flailing, like a net above my head,
His pounding heart is beating red.
THAT KISS tells **ALL** or just enough
To keep me Interested in **ALL** of his stuff.

Lips full of feelings, **THAT KISS**,
Soft as rose petals, free of prickly thorns.
In the the dark recesses of his mouth,
I find my way by the light in his eyes,
His smile is real, there is no disguise.

Even though we just met,
I am caught in the tangled web of
A hot-blooded, Israeli-Englishman:
"A Jack of All of Love's Trades."
A rare mixed-breed, a British accent,
Concealing a *Sabra, wherever he went.
Tricks of my own trade, I roll up my sleeve,
And I become a woman-in-need(?)
THAT KISS I can't forget, and with no regret:
It is almost 4 a.m., and inside of my gypsy's tent:
Sm(**OO**)ch, sm(**OO**)ch,
We are still one silhouette.

ANIMAL MAGNETISM:
Sm(**OO**)ch, sm(**OO**)ch,
Some call it v(**OO**)d(**OO**),
Most think it witchcraft,
Experts refer to it as "osculation."
Others call **THAT KISS** Kabbalah;
A kind of Jewish mysticism:
Many are in need of exorcism.

Translation: "Sabra" is a Jew born in Israel.

Sharon Esther Lampert
Sexiest Creative Genius in Human History
8th Prophetess of Israel: 22 Commandments
Todah Rabah to My Darling Muse Y.J. Jacks
© January 2003, All Rights Reserved.
www.PoetryJewels.com
Diamonds, Emeralds, Sapphires, Rubies, and Pearls

SEE THE WORLD THROUGH THE EYES OF A CREATIVE GENIUS
CUPID By Sharon Esther Lampert

Step 1. Connection On the last cold rainy day of winter, lingering on into the month of May, we meet in the middle of a street. He knows my first name, but not my last and we can't remember how we met. Every creature on earth is meeting, greeting, and preening. Mother nature is the matchmaker, the yenta busybody who has set the trap. I am cold, in need of a sweater and a warm heart and hand to hold. I am both vulnerable and vixen, a vessel Ready to be boarded by a seafaring sailor.

Step 2. Chemistry We stop and stare.
He is tall and handsome.
He is warm and inviting.
We have dinner at Tiny Thai.
I warm up on hot sake and Tom Kha Gai soup.
We celebrate his belated birthday.
We stop at Starbucks for decaffeinated tea, and share a chocolate brownie and kisses.
His heart is open and his arms are strong.
Unlike Cinderella, at the stroke of midnight I am lost in his embrace, drinking his sweet Elixir of kisses. Two hearts are set aflame.

Step 3. Communication We talk about this that, and the other. It is impossible to know another person. How was your day? We take another trip to Peruvian Pio Pio for a belated (May 9th) Cinco de Mayo celebration (May 5th). We have become world travelers. At this juncture in time, I at least know who I am. We celebrate his good fortune. We explore Six Handles, the most popular Frozen yogurt joint of sweet confections. We share dessert to maintain our figures. He likes hard ice cream. His favorite is Rocky Road. We are full but a hunger for love lingers. We share a non-caloric kiss, and then another. The world disappears into the background. Neighbors feel the love emanating from our embrace and shout out, "It's true love." His hand has taken hold of my magnificent breast. The passion between us is spreading like a raging wildfire, uncontainable.

Step 4. Common Ground
We love learning new things.
He is signed up for a non-credit course.
My mind is a private university where he can enroll and take a class.

Step 5. Comfortable
He is like a plush teddy bear on the outside. but on the interior insecurities are percolating. Demons dance to defeat. He is still single, in search of a sacred sanctuary built for two.
I am a "special-needs child." My gifts are my glory.

Step 6. Complexity
Intimacy is a complex equation of compound variables: mind, body, and spirit.
Quote: "You get everything you want and don't want in the same person."
I want to be a man's third wife. The first wife is a slave. The second wife is another failed attempt to get it right. By the third wife, he has given up, time is running out, and he wants to enjoy what time is left, my perfect guy.

© 2013 Book Excerpt
TRUE LOVE
SUCCESS STRATEGY
TrueLoveBurnsEternal.com

Soulmate Checklist
Do You Have Your Soulmate?

True Love Burns Eternal
Connection
Chemistry
Communication
Common Ground
Comfortable
Complexity
Compatibility
Companionship
Compromise
Collaboration
Change
Control
Conflict
Conditional Love
Crisis
Culture
Carefree
Contentment
Commitment
Celebration
Creativity
Consummation
Complex Equation
Compound Variables
Contribution or
Contamination?
Constructive Criticism
Cold Somebody
Curse
Crazy
Consciousness

"The Sole Intention of My Poetry Is to Add LIGHT to Your Soul"

SHARON ESTHER LAMPERT
'A' Listed
As One of the
World's Greatest Poets
www.worldfamouspoems.com

Step 7. Compatibility "We Just Clicked"
I am Leo the lioness. He is Taurus, the bull.
We are both fixed organizers (stubborn).
I am positive masculine. I am the Sun.
He is negative feminine. He is Venus.
I am fire, adding LIGHT, making things grow.
He is earth: tactile, stable, sensual, and erotic.
I am a QUEEN. We are both the boss and bossy.
We are destined for a collision, a battle of wills in the boardroom, not the bedroom.
Quote:"Opposites don't attract, they attack."

Step 8. Companionship: "Friends first and forever."
Date, one night stand, lover, friend, playmate, boyfriend or husband? I enjoy dating and having a playmate who loves N.Y.C. nightlife: Broadway, ballet, concerts, museums, sports, and travel.
"Solitude Is a blessing;loneliness Is a curse."

Step 9. Compromise: I,You,We
3 LIVES is the formula for success: Mine, Yours, and Ours.

Step 10. Collaboration
Can "WE" work together sharing responsibilities of raising a family? Or building a home or a business?

Step 11. Change Can he grow, ripen, and mature? Or is he set in his ways, a dinosaur on the verge of extinction?

Step 12. Control Can we share control? Boss or Bossy?
I want control of her... Is marriage a relic of a bygone era of subordination of women as servants and servitude?

Step 13. Conflict Can we negotiate a fair resolution in an unfair world? The "BLAME GAME" is not a solution to a problem. Do you Criticise or Compliment? Do you Contaminate or Contribute?

Step 14. Conditional Love Adult love is 100% conditional.
"You don't find love, you create love," "Most people don't love you; they love only what they want from you," "Most people don't have enough love for self-love, let alone to love you," "True Love Is Unconditional," and "Self-Love Is True Love."

Step 15. Crisis
99.9% Are Love-Hate Relationships because ... "All people help you with their strengths and hurt you with their weaknesses" (no exceptions to this rule) ... **"A warm nobody is better than a cold somebody"**... so **"Love Me or Leave Me."**

Step 16. Culture Generation Sexual Gratification: 75% Infidelity
- "Sex First. Love Maybe. Marriage Never."
- "Hot Sex Forever; Married Sex No More."
- "Single & Lonely, Married & Miserable, or Divorced & Bitter"
- "Friends with Benefits"

Step 17. Carefree (Are you learning, laughing, and loving?)
I am not trying to get into or out of a relationship.
I am just trying to enjoy the date, Mr. Right Now.

Steps 18 & 19. Contentment & Commitment
Q: Is he here for a reason, a season, or a lifetime?
Q: Is his heart, mind, and penis moving in the same direction?
Q: Is he a soft place to fall?
Q: Are joys doubled & sorrows halved? If so, he is a **keeper**.
"A loveless marriage is the loneliest place in the world."

Step 20. Celebration (Crazy and Consciousness)
Everything in life has a lifespan and an expiration date. The loss of true love is excruciating, and time does not heal the wound. Gratitude Is happiness. C*elebrate* each day, as if it were your last. In an INSANE world, your **C**RAZY and his **C**RAZY have to align.

Steps 21 & 22. Soulmate: Creativity & Consummation
I am a creative genius in need of a MUSE who can set my extra-body part, my "Creative Apparatus" on FIRE.
Quote: "I am a test of a man's virility." Touch me and live forever in my poem. **Immortality Is Mine And Yours.**
Dust to dust, except for this poem that educates, enlightens, entertains, and empowers. Energetic and magnetic, place poem in pocket to find your SOULMATE. Happy Birthday Steven.

For My Love, Dr. J.P.M., Harvard M.D., Lebanese-Half Jewish

My Man

Making Love All Through the—Night—
and Making Love All Through the—Day

My Man
is passionate and strong, all through
the night—I know his emotional,
spiritual, and physical being; I feel
the breadth and depth of his masculinity

All through the night, **My Man** holds
me tightly in his arms: warm, tender,
and cuddly—childlike—always knowing
where I am, secure forevermore

My Man's touch lingers—
I am sleeping soundly all
through the night, still making
love with him, in my dreams

I awaken to **My Man's** soft kisses at
dawn, my spirit floating in the morning
mist—the promise of love is fulfilled—
my heart is murmuring a melody, a
sweet new song, all through the day

By Sharon Esther Lampert

Remo "Drink, Drink, Drink"

(1) At Quattro Gatti, she is the poet-in-residence:
In Barcelona, Piccasso started here, painting
A humble sketch of a picket-white fence.

(2) Remo: His speciality, a watermelon martini.
Filling her glass to the very brim,
He closes the doors, and the lights dim.

"Drink, drink, drink," He commands!

(3) A dark Italian stallion, no doubt,
He pulls her bar stool closer to him,
Experienced in lust, he knows the route.

"Drink, drink, drink," He commands!

(4) Before his eyes, he sees only a red flower,
And takes a whiff, along her long stemmed neck,
He breathes her scent in, and is ready to devour…

"Drink, drink, drink," He commands!

(5) He longs for, and savors, a passionate kiss.
Skin soft like petals, and breasts ripe and firm
As rosebuds in bloom: it is after-working hours,
And he only has time to uproot the table flowers.

(6) However, rumors abound: the waiters resound.
For an extra tip, they will spin a tale of love, quite profound:

(7) Most say that he made love to her on top of his bar.
They say: She knocked over a glass, and still bears a scar.
Many agree that they made the bar their bed,
Leaving red lipstick stains painted in red.
Some say, they fell off their bar stools onto the floor
The neighbor next door says, he heard Remo roar.

(8) Others say that they have the love story all wrong!
At Quattro Gatti, she is the poet-in-residence:
So making love to her on his bar,
Or taking her home in his car,
Is taking the romantic fantasy too far.

(9) However, lingering in his air: a telltale sign.
He knows exactly where she is sitting,
Familiar with her perfumed scent, forevermore,
Whenever she enters his particular door.

(10) The truth of their encounter, lives on in one of the four
Cats, sitting still on the window sill, wearing the bell:
One saw, one heard, one dreamt, and one played,
And loyal to their Master Remo, they will never tell.

EPIC
Love Ever Reborn Is Ever Ever Newborn
By Sharon Esther Lampert

(1)
Driven by ever Delectable Delights of
Pure Perfections of Sweet-Skin Confections
Ever Enamoured
Sinewy Soft Skins Embrace
Ever Enkindled
Warm ever Tender Kisses ever Feverish Touching ever Retouching
Ever Entangled
Two Naked Souls are ever Woven as ever One
Ever Entwined
Ever Head To Head ever Heart To Heart ever Toe To Toe
Ever Engulfed
Caresses ever Consume ever Conquering evermore
Ever Enraptured
Ever Emotional, ever Physical, ever Spiritual, ever Divine
Love ever Reborn is Love ever Newborn

(2)
Ever Enlaced
Ever Fine Cottony Linens and Ever Plush Pillows Harbor an
Ever Enchanted
Tribal Princess of Israel
Ever An Entourage
Ever Emanating
Fanciful Artistic Persuasions and
Ever Enmeshed
Ever Enthroned is a
French Speaking Lebanese King of
Ever Endowed
Virtuous Virility and
Kind Keeper of Medicinal Powers of the ever Sacred Heart
Ever Enobled
Two Intensities of Two Beings are ever United as Each Other's Beloved
Love ever Reborn is Love ever Newborn

(3)
Ever Enveloped
Tightly Bound From Dusk Till Dawn Lovers Inextricably Embrace
Ever Enveloped
Touchingly By Osmosis Powerful Emotions Permeate Satin Skins
Ever Enveloped
Ever Thrusting ever Churning to Mysterious Musical Muses
Ever Enveloped
Full Bodied Naked Souls Ferment in Infinite Emotional Depths
Ever Enveloped
Cloaked by Romantic Fantasies Desires Seductively Impel
Ever Enveloped
Thresholds of ever Towering Peaks of ever Tremendous Passions ever Arise
Ever Enveloped
Two Hearts Secure in an ever Sacred Union ever Harmonizing
Ever Enveloped
Ever Needing to be ever Accepted ever Cherished ever Unconditionally
Ever Enveloped
Two Together ever Feasting as One ever Body ever Mind ever Soul
Love ever Reborn is Love ever Newborn.
Ever Drawing Nearer . . . and ever Closer
Enticing, Ecstasy is ever Unabridged

(4)
Ever Drawing Nearer . . . and ever Closer
Enthalled, Ecstasy is ever Unbounded
Ever Drawing Nearer . . . and ever Closer
Enraptured, Ecstasy is ever Unbridled
Love ever Reborn is Love ever Newborn

(5)
Ever Ecstatic
Love is ever Reborn
In Yesterday's Daring Darknesses of the Deepening Night
Ever Exalted
Love is ever Reborn
In between the Slumber of One Sleepless Night And One Dreamy Day
Ever Exuberant
Love is ever Reborn
In Tomorrow's Penetrating Spiked Peaks of a Parting Sunrise
Love ever Reborn is Love ever Newborn

(6)
Ever Effervescent
Lit By Catalytic Sunlight of the New Day
Lovers Separate
Ever Resolved and ever Unresolved
Ever Enriched
In ever Body ever Mind ever Soul
Love Rehomogenizes
Ever Resolved and ever Unresolved
Ever Enlightened
In a Love for the Self and a Love for the Other
Love Separates
Ever Resolved and ever Unresolved
Love ever Reborn is Love ever Newborn

(7)
Ever Returning
An Enduring Hunger Remains
Ever Unforgettable
In Complete Recall
Ever Enshrined
In Eternally Memorable Time
Ever Endless
Love ever Never ever Ceasing
Ever Entrusted
Promising to Love All-Ways in ever Time ever Touch ever Intensity
Love ever Reborn is Love ever Newborn

(8)
Ever Entwined in ever Endless Pretzels ever Unending
ever Intimacy ever Uninhibited,
ever Intimacy ever Unencumbered,
ever Intimacy ever Uncontaminated,
ever Hard, ever Longing for Physical
Recovery, ever Wanting to Begin Again,
the Music of His Beating Heart, His Lips,
His Hands, the Blankets ever Unfurling
Love ever Reborn is Love ever Newborn

(9)
Ever Enterprising
In a Grand Kingdom of Majestic Brownstone
Filled with Funnel Shaped Ruby Red Gladiolus
Ever Mightier Kingdoms within the
Ever Mightiest Kingdoms are
Ever Awaiting to be ever Awakened
Ever Enduring
Built by the Creator of
Ever Eternal Divinity and
Ever Eternal Desire

(10)
Ever Enshrouded
Ever Flowering Bi-Petals
Ever Decorate the
Ever Opening
Ever Widening
Ever Ascending
Opulent Pearly Ever Pink
Velvet Lipped Vestibule of
Ever Insatiable Pleasure

(11)
Ever an Enigma
Oilwells
Ever Gushing
Ever Liquid
Ever Lasting
Ever Lingering
Ever the Starry Night

(12)
Ever Entitled
Secrets of Lubrication
Ever H20 Designs of Universal Forms:
Ever Green Salad, Moist Israeli Feta Cheese, and Lemon Dressing
Ever Warm Challah French Toast and Maple Syrup
Ever Crispy Cereal, Bananas, Chile Blueberries, and Cold Milk
Ever Hard Red Brick and Creamy Wet Cement
Ever Fast Sports Cars and Premium Oils
Ever Touch, ever Time, and ever Intensity

(13)
Ever Engorged
Ever Echoing in the Palace of
Ever Erect Grandeur
Symphonies of
Ever Roarrrring Climactic Orgasm
Ever Resounds in
Ever - Perrrrfected -
Ever Form Fitting Intercourse
Love ever Reborn is Love ever Newborn.

(14)
Ever Encompassed
Powerful Tunnels of
Varying Dimensions
Harbor Mysterious
Side by Side
Channels of Deepening Crevices
Ever Canyons of Carnivals:

(15)
Ever an Encore
By ever Cosmic Conception
Dramas of Devastating Death and
Miraculous Rebirths ever Re-Play on the
Stage of the Womb

(16)
Ever Enacted
The Egg Actress and
Sperm Actors
Ever Cling as
Ever Upstream Heroes to
Rescue the
Ever Encapsulated
Doomed Egg Heroine

(17)
Ever An Ensemble
Moonlit Serenades
Ever Monthly
Ever Ensheathed
Messssssssssssy
Menstruation of an Egg's Death
Cycle after Cycle
Play On and On

(18)
Ever Ephemeral
A 9 Month Pregnancy for
Evolvvvvvvvvvving
New Evolutionary
Beings
Ever Ensued
Nausssssssssssseating
Vomit of Conception

(19)
Ever Enwombed
Excruuuuuuuuuciatingly
Painful Joyous Birth and
Ever Rebirths Replay

(20)
Ever Enwinding
A Sustaining Umbilical Cord is Severed
Ever Enwrapped
A Nutritious Placenta is Discarded
Ever Enclosed
Disposables of
Biological Love Waste

(21)
Ever Enabled
A Newborn
Ever Reborn
Independently is
Ever Born
Anew
Dependent
Ever Unabled

(22)
Ever Ensouled
Love is Bound Up
Ever to be Reborn as an
Ever Beloved Newborn
Ever Ensphered
In Destiny
Ever after ever and ever Forever

Unleash The Creator The God Within

I was born gifted. It is a gift that keeps giving!

I refer to my extra body part as my "**C**reative **A**pparatus."

My gift is my most important relationship, my most rewarding relationship, and paradoxically, my most difficult relationship:

EXCITING! EXHILERATING! ELECTRIFYING! EXHAUSTING!

I awake in the middle of a sleepless night and write the whole book! —There are no rough drafts!

I am no longer an I — I am a WE — or maybe a THEY?

My gift did not come with an instruction manual. There were no teachers to guide me, and no classes to teach how to maximize my creative potential.

Intuitive gifts of insight, imagination, and vision cannot be taught in school.

I am its servant and messenger, and the instrument of its desires and destiny!

Sharon Esther Lampert
SEE THE WORLD THROUGH THE EYES OF A CREATIVE GENIUS
Poet, Philosopher, Prophet, Peacemaker, Princess & Pea, Paladin of Education, and Prodigy

"I was born with an extra-body part called a creative apparatus. My left eye is a human telescope and my right eye is a human microscope. I can see the big picture and the small details. My mind is a private university of infinite departments: Poety, philosophy, education, theology, music, arts, and pop culture. I bring new information into the world."

Microscope: My Right Eye

Telescope: My Left Eye

V.E.S.S.E.L.
Very Extra Special Sharon Esther Lampert

An Artist Marches to the Beat of a Different Drummer.
Sharon Esther Lampert Marches to the Beats of an Orchestra.

NYU Honored **Sharon Esther Lampert** with an Award for "Multi-Interdisciplinary Studies" (YOUTUBE video)

Poet: World Famous Poems
Prophet: 22 Commandments
Philosopher Queen
Peacemaker: World Peace Equation
Princess & Pea
PINUP
Performer: Vocalist
Player: Jock, NYU Varsity
Paladin of Education
PHOTON SUPERHERO
Princess Kadimah
8TH Prophetess of Israel
President
Publisher
Producer
Psychobiologist: Rockefeller University
Piano-Playing Cat
Phoenix
Prodigy

My Websites:

SharonEstherLampert.com
PhilosopherQueen.com
WorldFamousPoems.com
PoetryJewels.com
GodIsGoDo.com
Schmaltzy.com
TrueLoveBurnsEternal.com
SillyLittleBoys.com
Smartgrades.com
EverydayanEasyA.com
PhotonSuperHero.com
BooksNotBombs.com
WritersRunTheWorld.com
PalmBeachBookPublisher.com
MiamiBookPublisher.com
HappyGrandparenting.com
BooksArePowerful.com
WinAtThin.com
WomenHaveAllThePower.com

SEE THE WORLD THROUGH THE EYES OF A CREATIVE GENIUS

About the Prodigy

SHARON ESTHER LAMPERT

V.E.S.S.E.L. **V**ery. **E**xtra. **S**pecial. **S**haron. **E**sther. **L**ampert.

POET — One of the World's Greatest Poets "A LIST"
World Poetry Record: 120 Words of Rhyme from One Family of Rhyme
Greatest Poems Ever Written on Extraordinary World Events

http://famouspoetsandpoems.com/poets.html

PRODIGY

- Unleash the Creator, The God Within: 10 Esoteric Laws of Genius and Creativity

PROPHET — GOD IS GO! DO!

- The 22 Commandments: All You Will Ever Need to Know About God
- God Talks to Me: A Working Definition of God

PHILOSOPHER QUEEN

- Temporary Insanity: We Are All Building Our Lives on a Sand Trap—Written in Letter S
- God of What? Is Life a Gift or a Punishment? 10 Absolute Truths
- WOMEN HAVE ALL THE POWER But Have Never Learned How to Use It!
- Sperm Manifesto: 10 Rules for the Road

PEACEMAKER

World Peace Equation.com

PHOTON SUPERHERO OF EDUCATION

PALADIN OF EDUCATION

SMARTGRADES BRAIN POWER REVOLUTION
- "The Silent Crisis Destroying America's Brightest Minds"

BOOK OF THE MONTH, Alma Public Library, Wisconsin
- EVERYDAY AN EASY A.com
- 40 Universal Gold Standards of Education
- Intra-personal Integration Therapy
- 15 Stepping Stones of Academic Successs
- 15 Stumbling Blocks of Academic Failure

Pioneer

- SILLY LITTLE BOYS: 40 Rules of Manhood, sillylittleboys.com
- LYMTY: Love You More Than Yesterday
  14 Relationship Strategies for Happily Ever After
- In One Hour, Read Hebrew
- CUPID: The Language of Love—Written in Letter C
- Publish: The Secret Sauce of Book Sales—Written in Letter P
- Win at Thin: Fat Me, Skinny Me—Written in Letter A

PIN-UP

SEXIEST CREATIVE GENIUS IN HUMAN HISTORY

Artists March to the Beat of a Different Drummer
Sharon Esther Lampert Marches to the Beat of an Entire Orchestra

Poet, Philosopher, Prophet
Paladin of Education, Peacemaker
Princess & Pea, Phoenix, PHOTON, PINUP, Prodigy

Big-Blue-Eyes. Brilliant Books. Beautiful & Buxom. Blessed.

Sharon Esther Lampert was born an **OLD SOUL**—She was never young! Sharon is a lefty.
At age nine, her mother declared: **"My daughter is a poet, philosopher, and teacher!"**
At age nine, Sharon was writing books on memo pads, and binding them together with a stapler.
When Sharon walked into a room, her mother would proclaim, "THE QUEEN HAS ARRIVED!"

Her mother nicknamed her daughter, **"The Princess and the Pea!"** Sharon's greatest literary works woke her up in the middle of the night — and made her get up out of bed— and write them down. Sharon writes an entire book in one night! e.g., GOD TALKS TO ME: A WORKING DEFINITION OF GOD

Sharon's literary genius is to amalgamate poetry, philosophy, and comedy into one sentence.
Sharon's BIG BRAIN conceptualizes BIG IDEAS using one letter of the alphabet: C, S, D and P.
Sharon's mother was the sole person in Sharon's life who knew who Sharon was from the INSIDE OUT! — and what would become of her.

Her beloved mother also knew to her very last breath... the exact day and to-the minute when she would die! (Eve Paikoff Lampert: June 3, 1925—May 5, 1985).

Sharon Esther's Gifts Are Metaphysical **— Beyond the Scope of Scientific Inquiry**

There Are No Rough Drafts! — My Books Write Themselves!
(There Are 4 Books with **God** in the Title)

"A LIST" Sharon Esther Lampert is One of the World's Greatest Poets
http://famouspoetsandpoems.com/poets.html

#1 Poetry Website for Student Projects
On a global scale, Sharon's poetry is used by teachers for their poetry lesson plans, and by students for their poetry projects.

New York University Awards (YOUTUBE Videos) **BA, MA, MA**

Sharon Esther earned three degrees from NYU — and she was honored with two NYU awards.
Sharon represented her class at her M.A. graduation — and was honored with an award for "Multi-Interdisciplinary Studies."
She also played on the NYU Women's Varsity Basketball Team as a Center in the $16 million Coles Sports Center.
Sharon won an "NYU Weightlifting Contest"— Sharon was the sole contestant — so she won! (NYU Washington Square News article).

"When I'm not writing, I'm reading. When I'm not writing or reading, I'm singing." (YOUTUBE videos).
—Sharon Esther Lampert

One of the World's Greatest Poets

http://famouspoetsandpoems.com/poets.html

List of Poets - Famous Poets and Poems   http://famouspoetsandpoems.com/poets.html

 Larry Levis (3) (1946 - 1996)

 Amy Levy (69) (1861 - 1889)

 Louise Labe (1) (1524 - 1566)

 David Lehman (58) (1948 - present)

 Jiri Mordecai Langer (1) (1894 - 1943)

 John Lindley (4) (1952 - present)

 Dimitris Lyacos (3) (1966 - present)

 Yahia Lababidi (10) (1973 - present)

 Laurie Lee (6) (1914 - 1997)

 Walter Savage Landor (52) (1775 - 1864)

 Michael Lally (1) (1942 - present)

 Major Henry Livingston, Jr. (23) (1748 - 1828)

 Roddy Lumsden (2) (1966 - present)

 Sharmagne Leland-St. John (5) (1953 - present)

 Sharon Esther Lampert (19) (0 - present)

M

 Claude McKay (76) (1889 - 1948)

 Spike Milligan (35) (1918 - 2002)

 Marianne Moore (18) (1887 - 1972)

 John Milton (102) (1608 - 1674)

 A. A. Milne (22) (1882 - 1956)

 Czeslaw Milosz (33) (1911 - 2004)

 Edgar Lee Masters (251) (1868 - 1950)

 William Matthews (10) (1942 - 1997)

 Edwin Muir (14) (1887 - 1959)

 Roger McGough (14) (1937 - present)

 Walter de la Mare (44) (1873 - 1956)

 Antonio Machado (8) (1875 - 1939)

 Edna St. Vincent Millay (165) (1892 - 1950)

 W. S. Merwin (23) (1927 - present)

 John Masefield (25) (1878 - 1967)

 Louis MacNeice (3) (1907 - 1963)

 Thomas Moore (144) (1779 - 1852)

 Christopher Marlowe (6) (1564 - 1593)

What Happens When You Dress Up Albert Einstein As Marilyn Monroe?
SHARON ESTHER LAMPERT

SEE THE WORLD THROUGH THE EYES OF A CREATIVE GENIUS

FAN MAIL
FANS@SharonEstherLampert.com

FAN MAIL
FANS@SharonEstherLampert.com

A PHENOMENON...
SHARON ESTHER LAMPERT

Lithe and lovely ... like a fawn.
This lady fascinates me ... from dusk till dawn.
Feminine and comely ... she's beyond belief
A blue-beam from her eyes ... is my soothing relief.

Girlish in her braces ... maidenly in her style
I yearn for her embraces ... and adore her friendly smile.
As tasteful as any artist ... you'll ever see
She's a compendium of class ... from A to Z.

If you'd like to see a figure, that puts Venus to shame
Behold her in a swimsuit, and your passions will aflame.
Ever exuding goodness . . . guided from above
Miss Sharon is the essence, and epitome of Love.

She's the inspiration of sages, and also fools like me
And the most magnificent female, I'm sure I'll ever see.
The nights are now endearing, & never filled with doubt
I sometimes wake up singing, cause it's Sharon . . .
I dream about.

Affectionately, . .
A devoted fan,
—Harry McVeety

FAN MAIL
FANS@SharonEstherLampert.com

Well they are beautiful poems and wonderful writings.
I did go to poetry jewels today, but I confess, mainly to look at your legs.
Shabbat Shalom.
—Bernstein

Dear Princess Kadimah:
Thank you for putting your poetry on the net, especially the one about dating an Israeli man. It helped me sort out a date I had Saturday with an Israeli (former military soldier, of course). Jewish guys always lunge at me, but this one was more like a missile. I don't know where to file this experience.
Thanks,
—Kim

Sharon ("Kadimah"),
I just visited your website. Amazing! Your work is profound, prolific, and so beautifully poetic. Your beautiful and gentle soul seems so transparent through your writings. Your intellect abounds. I would love to know more...
I'd love to hear from you.
Warmly,
—David

... Moves me deeply. It's so rare to see such a physically beautiful, and spiritually profound, person on the net.
—AH Aaron Henry

December, 22, 2000
Thank you for letting me know of your poem. Edith Stein was a great and important person and it is good to know that she is being heard again.
—Paul

Paul Douglas Stamm
Technology Coordinator
Divine Savior Holy Angels High School
4257 N. 100th Street
Milwaukee, WI 53222
www.dsha.k12.wi.us

FAN MAIL
FANS@SharonEstherLampert.com

Dear Sharon,

You are not only an exquisite poet, you're beautiful! Am smitten by your luminous beingness. Are you an angel in disguise--a so-called malachim in Hebrew if I am not mistaken.

Thank you for your wondeful open-hearted response.

Your photo will sit next to those of Gautama Buddha and the Blessed Virgin Mary.

I will follow your sound esoteric advise regarding the positioning of your photo and the two other icons.

I am deeply impressed that you are very conscious about the concept of sacred space and the flow of spiritual energy.

So please send me your precious photo as soon as possible.

P.S. Will you be generous enough to send me your signed photo which I will place on the secret altar of my heart, lit by the menorah, the seven-stemmed candelabra of your inspiration, O mystical muse, O Rose of Sharon...

Your ardent fan and admirer,

—Felix Fojas, the cybercat with a mystical meow
Chico, CA, 95926

FAN MAIL
FANS@SharonEstherLampert.com

Congregation Emanu-El
of the City of New York
Fifth Avenue at Sixty-fifth Street
New York, N.Y. 10021-6596

Study of
DAVID M. POSNER

September 22, 1999

The New York Public Library
Humanities and Social Sciences Library
Fifth Avenue and 42nd Street
New York, NY 10018-2788

Dear Friends:

Sharon Esther Lampert has made application for a fellowship from the Center for Scholars and Writers. It is with greatest pleasure that I write to you in support of her application.

I can best describe this remarkable woman by citing the analysis of Moses Maimonides, in his "Guide for the Perplexed," concerning psychological endowments. He noted the class of people who are intellectually superior, but whose imaginative faculties are deficient. These, he said, were philosophers. Then there are those whose imaginative faculties are highly developed, but who are deficient intellectually. He said these are dreamers and politicians. But then he observed the rare people who have both highly developed intellects and imaginations. These, he said, are prophets.

Sharon Esther Lampert falls into the last category. She has one of the most gifted intellects I have ever encountered, and her imaginative capacity is absolutely awesome.

I have known many people throughout my long career at Temple Emanu-El. I have never met anyone like this extraordinary human being.

Again, awesome is the most appropriate word.

Yours truly,

[signature]

FORMED BY THE CONSOLIDATION OF EMANU-EL CONGREGATION AND TEMPLE BETH-EL

#1 Poetry Website
for Student Projects

FAN MAIL
FANS@SharonEstherLampert.com

Windsor High School
6208 Hwy 61-67
Imperial, Mo 63052

SAINT LOUIS MO 631
27 MAY 05 PM

Sharon Esther Lampert
P.O.BOX 103,
New York, New York, 10028, US

Cody Howell
1042 Prospect Dr.
Imperial, Mo 63052
May 2, 2005

Sharon Esther Lampert
P.O.BOX 103,
New York, New York,10028,US

Dear, Sharon E. Lampert

Hello, My name in Cody, I am a Junior at Windsor High School in Missouri. I have had the chance to write to any one person and I picked you. I have always enjoyed quotes and sayings. Theirs just something about it, like I have always known there is a "better way" but never really found anything until I started to pay attention that their was more than just physical happenings. The poet has the ability to drink from streams science has yet to discover. I used to always reads one liners like
" a community begins to grow when old men plant trees they know they will never enjoy the shade of." Things like this really interested me. Something more than what I had known.

    I am very curious by nature, and this kind of wisdom/intellect really hit the spot for me, now I have many poems, sayings, quotes ext. I can't recite them by heart but I thourouly enjoyed the ones I read. I didn't know of you until me and my buddy were talking about how we like psychology and basically more than average and the "better way". After reading some of your quotes I realized you must have seen your share of happenings and become very wise over the years of thought, poetry, and life.

    My first thought was to write to you and try to flatter you because I enjoyed your work. Well I guess you made your poetry your work. Then I started thinking that this well of knowledge , all that stuff you've learned, it would be a long shot but my curiosity wouldn't stop unless if I asked you if you could share some of the knowledge you have gained. Any and all would be appreciated and probably useful later considering I am still just a 17-year-old kid. I can't think of any other word than greedy, but you have already thought so many with your influences, and I ask you to help me out, If your busy you have already done more than enough, thank you, and thanks for your time while reading this. I am sorry but I always find myself looking for more and I'm positive you have gained useful info in your day. I could imagine the child who has heard many stories, lesions, and wisdoms of many. He'd be one of the most diverse ,intelligent humans around, and with something like this in mind how could I not be greedy.

    I have already learned some from Internet, friends like the one who told me about poems, and family. I have tried to learn patience from the impatient, kindness from the angry, and truth from fools, but for some reason I'm not thankful for these teachers. I still feel as if I could have more, and the lessons of an older experienced poet just has something about how it sounds. Greatness is all I've seen come from poets their ability to make one think is amazing , I could just imagine the wisdom of an experienced one.

    Either way I just wanted to say thank you for your time and thank you for doing what you have done. Your shared wisdom and lessons will help many and your work might not be remembered forever but I believe that your positive effect will. Thank you again

    Your student ,
    Cody

Date: Thursday, November 19, 2009, 3:11 PM

Dear Ms. Lampert,
I am working on a poetry project for my senior English class. Instead of a boring research paper we are to analyze a famous poet and make a power point, and a creative presentation over the poets life, work and also criticisms of their work. The last part is the problem, I can't seem to find any scholarly criticisms of your work. Do you know of any, or have on record any criticisms of your work, either oral or written? My project partner and I would love to do our project on you because we find you very interesting and your poems very in tune with the lives of people today and the problems we face as modern people. Any help would be appreciated.
Thank you again.
Sincerely,
—Michael Rockey

Date: April 10, 2009 6:15:32 PM

Hi Sharon!
My name is Alexa & I'm a junior in high school! I love your poems, especially about world affairs. I will be doing a poetry analysis on three of your poems **(I've chosen Sandstorm in Iraq, Tsunami, and There Is No Flower in Darfur)** and also a presentation to inform the class of your works, accomplishments & biography. I have been searching every website and library on some information about you, but can't find any! If you can it would be greatly appreciated if you could tell me a little about your childhood, parents, education, religious beliefs, and maybe some experiences that have shaped your views or positions in regards to your poetry!
Thanks so much!
Have an amazing day!
—Alexa Young

Date: January 20, 2010 9:54:04 PM

Hello Miss Lampert,
My name is Kal Marshall, I am a student at Johnson City High School, Johnson City, New York. I am currently enrolled in AP English and Literature. My teacher realized my classes misunderstanding for poetry and decided to have us write paper on a poem of our choice and about the poet. While searching the web for an interesting poem I came among yours and knew it was the poem I was meant to write a paper on. One part of the paper is to "Interview" someone who has read the poem. While I was on your website I found the little note about E-mailing you. So I was wondering if you would be willing to give me a little more detail on your poem, **"EDUCATE NOT."** From the basis under which it was derived from, to your true feeling and understanding of the poem, to how you feel about it now from when you were writing it. Your Bio is extremely interesting, and I hope to learn more. Thank you very much for creating a poem I could actually enjoy to spend a month working on. and hopefully I hear back from you in a reasonable time.
Thanks Again,
—Kal Marshall

THE SEXIEST CREATIVE GENIUS IN HUMAN HISTORY

Sharon Esther Lampert

Poet
Prophet
Philosopher
Peacemaker
Paladin of Education
Princess
Prodigy
Pin-Up

SEE THE WORLD THROUGH THE EYES OF A CREATIVE GENIUS

Gazillions...
National & International Poetry Publications

Afghanistan: RAHA
2003:
Princess Kadimah is Published in Afghanistan: RAHA
Dear Sharon
I added you to my list and also your work is published on the net:
http://rahapen.org/options_poetry_Sharon.htm
Regards
—Kamran Mirhazar
Raha PEN Club
Email: rahapen@kabulpress.org
0093-799390025
Kabul, Afghanistan: Post Box number: 3219

Dear Sharon Esther Lampert,
Your artistic poem CENTRAL PARK: Water Fight, Flight and Tears
marked by true creative genius,
has been published in the June of Taj Mahal Review an International
Literary Journal ISSN 0972-6004.
This Journal contains 300 pages of short stories,literary articles and
poems by authors from all over the world.
The Journal is an attempt to select the best of world poetry.
Best Wishes
—RADHA AGRAWAL
www.cyberwit.net
4/2 B, L.I.G.
Govindpur Colony Allahabad - 211004 (U.P.)
INDIA

Dear Sharon,
When we made our recent call for submissions, in which we asked for writings pertaining to the terrorist attacks of September 11, 2001, we were unsure what kind of response we would get. As it turns out, we have received poetry, fiction, and essays from writers all over the world. Our "feature writer section" for October will include the work of over 100 writers. We are very happy to include your work in this section. Your contribution to this project is an integral part of the overall tone and spirit of the October issue. We want to thank you for helping us in this project and, more importantly, expressing yourself at a time when to do so is both difficult and essential. Thank you again for sending us your work.
The October issue will come out on October 21, 2001.
 Sincerely,
The Pedestal Magazine
 www.thepedestalmagazine.com

Sharon, Thanks for the note. I really appreciate it. A gift, huh? Wow, I am intigued and flattered. By the way, several people really liked your writing in the current Pedestal. Best,
—John Amen

Gazillions...
National & International Poetry Publications

Dear Sharon,
Thank you so much for the kind comments.
I am pleased to have your poems Timeless Sandcastles and Sacred Feathers Of Divine Freedoms appearing in the first issue of Thought Fragments.
I will send you a reminder email when the first issue goes up.
Once again, thank you.
Best wishes,
—Darlene Zagata

Featured Poem of the Month:
Cool...thanks!
It's a pleasure to feature your work.
I want you to know that i have a lot of respect and admiration for Jewish people.
I look forward to learning more about you and your culture through your work.
—Nate

Dear Sharon,
Several weeks ago we informed you by mail that our editors wish to include your poetry in a new collection of poems written by the Best poets we have encountered. We need to hear back from you immediately if you wish to be included in the special edition . . .
The Best Poems and Poets of 2002
Library of Congress ISBN 0-7951-5175-6

Dear Sharon,
My name is August Highland - i am a writer and editor - i read your work
i dream forge - i like your work - a lot - i want to include your work in the next issue of
the little literary -journal of which i am the editor - you can see the muse apprentice
guild at www.muse-apprentice-guild.com - internet explorer 5.5 or higher is required
send me as many pieces as you like sharon and they can be of any
length - also include a short bio
Always,
—August

Dear Sharon,
We have discussed this at length and have concluded that your
poems are truly unique and rather exciting.
Fondly,
—Ruby M.
Editor, PrinsessTarta Magazine

Sharon,
How do we get your poem into my site?
—Richard Williams, Editor

World Famous Quotes

THERE IS ONE GLOBAL ENEMY: IGNORANCE
—PHOTON SUPERHERO OF EDUCATION

LONELINESS IS DEATH
SOLITUDE IS DIVINE
—Philosopher Queen Sharon Esther Lampert

BE HARD
ON A WOMAN ONLY WHEN MAKING LOVE TO HER
—Philosopher Queen Sharon Esther Lampert

FIGHT TO LIVE
LIVE TO FIGHT
BORN TO DIE
—Philosopher Queen Sharon Esther Lampert

THERE IS ONLY ONE TRUTH
NO ONE HAS THE TRUTH
—Philosopher Queen Sharon Esther Lampert

World Famous Quotes

It's Not Easy Being a Jewish Sex Symbol But Someone Has to Do It!

— Prodigy Sharon Esther Lampert

THE 11 COMMANDMENT
KEEP THEM LAUGHING KEEP THEM SANE

There Are 5 Books of Moses and 5000 Books of Jewish Comedy

—Princess Kadimah, 8TH Prophetess of Israel

GOD IS GO! DO!
God Can Only Do for You, What God Can Do Through You

God is Not Physics — The Laws of the Universe
God is Metaphysics! — Beyond the Scope of Scientific Inquiry
Like Mind, Thoughts, and Ideas — Beyond the Scope of Scientific Inquiry

—Prophet Sharon Esther Lampert

Less Than 1% Population & 22% of Nobel Prizes
Wherever Jews Go, Grass Grows
Wherever Israelis Go, Gardens Grow

—Princess Kadimah, 8TH Prophetess of Israel

KADIMAH PRESS: *Gifts of Genius*

REVELATIONS! MY BOOKS WRITE THEMSELVES!

Poet: The Greatest Poems Ever Written on Extraordinary World Events
Title: I Stole All the Words from the Dictionary
#1 Poetry Website for School Projects
A List: One of the World's Greatest Poets
ISBN Hardcover: 978-1-885872-06-7
ISBN Paperback: 978-1-885872-07-4
ISBN E-Book: 978-1-885872-08-1

Prodigy: WORLD PREMIERE!
Title: Unleash the Creator The God Within
10 Esoteric Laws of Genius and Creativity
ISBN Hardcover: 978-1-885872-21-0
ISBN Paperback: 978-1-885872-22-7
ISBN E-Book: 978-1-885872-23-4

Prophet: WORLD PREMIERE! **GOD IS GO! DO!**
Title: GOD TALKS TO ME: A WORKING DEFINITION OF GOD
ISBN Hardcover: 978-1-885872-33-3
ISBN Paperback: 978-1-885872-34-0
ISBN E-Book: 978-1-885872-36-4

Prophet: WORLD PREMIERE!
Title: The 22 Commandments: All You Will Ever Need to Know About God
A Universal Moral Compass For All People, For All Religions, For All Time
ISBN Hardcover: 978-1-885872-03-6
ISBN Paperback: 978-1-885872-04-3
ISBN E-Book: 978-1-885872-05-0

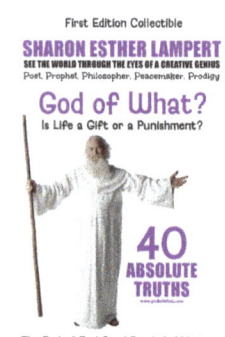

Philosopher: WORLD PREMIERE!
Title: God of What? Is Life a Gift or a Punishment? 10 Absolute Truths
ISBN Hardcover: 978-1-885872-00-5
ISBN Paperback: 978-1-885872-01-2
ISBN E-Book: 978-1-885872-02-9
GodofWhat.com

KADIMAH PRESS: Gifts of Genius

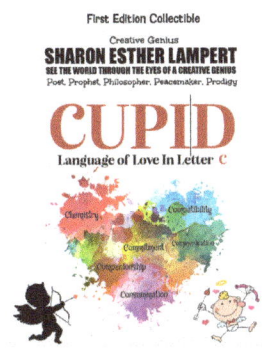

Prodigy: WORLD PREMIERE!
Title: CUPID: Language of Love—Written in Letter C
ISBN Hardcover: 978-1-885872-55-5
ISBN Paperback: 978-1-885872-56-2
ISBN E-Book: 978-1-885872-57-9
SharonEstherLampert.com

Prodigy: WORLD PREMIERE!
Title: TEMPORARY INSANITY
We Are All Building Our Lives on a Sand Trap- Written in Letter S
ISBN Hardcover: 978-1-885872-70-8
ISBN E-Book: 978-1-885872-71-5
SharonEstherLampert.com

Popular: Children's Book, Ages 8-12
Title: SCHMALTZY: IN AMERICA, EVEN A CAT CAN HAVE A DREAM
ISBN Hardcover: 978-1-885872-39-5
ISBN Paperback: 978-1-885872-38-8
ISBN E-Book: 978-1-885872-37-1
Schmaltzy.com

Color-Coded Vocabulary Words

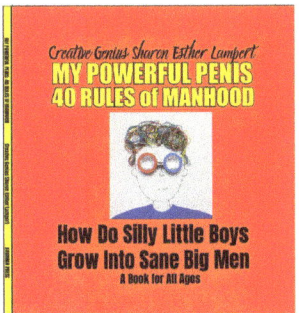

Popular: WORLD PREMIERE
Title: 40 RULES OF MANHOOD - WORLD PREMIERE!
HOW DO SILLY LITTLE BOYS GROW INTO SANE BIG MEN
14 Global Catastrophes of Violence Against Women
ISBN Hardcover: 978-1-885872-29-6
ISBN Paperback: 978-1-885872-35-7
ISBN E-Book: 978-1-885872-41-8
SillyLittleBoys.com

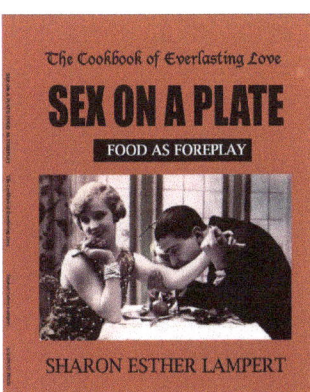

Popular: Every Relationship Begins with a Great Meal
Title: SEX ON A PLATE: FOOD AS FOREPLAY
THE COOKBOOK OF EVERLASTING LOVE
ISBN Hardcover: 978-1-885872-46-3
ISBN Paperback: 978-1-885872-48-7
ISBN E-Book: 978-1-885872-47-0
TrueLoveBurnsEternal.com

Count Your Blessings. Practice Gratitude

"Never Underestimate the Power of a Girl with a Book"
—ICON Supreme-Court Justice Ruth Bader Ginsburg

1. MY Genetic Gift of Genius
- Lefty: Born with an Extra Body Part: "Creative Apparatus"
- Two Sets of Artsy-Fartsy Genes: Maternal Grandfather Benjamin Paikoff and Father Abraham Lampert
- Vocalist: Ashira Orchestra (YOUTUBE videos)
- Athlete: NYU Women's Varsity Basketball Team

2. MY LIFE: Dawn of Digital Revolution
- The Golden Age of Personal Computers: APPLE
- The Golden Age of Creativity: ADOBE
- The Golden Age of Email, Internet, and Globalization

NYU President Andrew Hamilton and Me

NYU Special Mention
NYU President John Brademas (backed his limosine into my bicycle)
Professor Yael Feldman (the writer's relationship to MOMMY)
Professor Paul Humphreys (family therapy)
Professor Ted Coons, (my position at Rockefeller University)
John, The Security Guard at Coles Sports Center (SUPERFAN)
B-Ball Coaches: Evelyn Hannon and Sherri Pickard

3. MY LOVED ONES:
- UNCONDITIONAL TRUE LOVE: MOMMY
- My PURRfect Children: SCHMALTZY & FALAFEL, Schmaltzy.com (YOUTUBE videos)
- My Muse: NYU Professor Karl Bardosh "Friends First and Forever and Family"
- My Metaphysical Sister: Poet Hannah Szenes: "ELI, ELI"
- My 7 Practice Husbands, Muses, and Dates

4. MY EDUCATION: BA, MA, MA and Awards (YOUTUBE videos)
- NYU MENTOR: Laurin Raiken: NYU **"Multi-Interdisciplinary Award"** and **M.A. Class Representative**
- ROCKEFELLER UNIVERSITY, NYC, Publication: "Hyperphagia and Obesity Induced by Neuropeptide Y"
- 100-Year Scholarship Award Winner, Presented by NYC Mayor Edward Koch
- Empire Science Scholarship Award Winner
- Jerusalem Fellowship Award of Aish Hatorah
- Won a Weightlifting Contest, NYU Coles Sports Center (Washington Square News)

5. MY SPORTS:
- N.Y.C. Marathon
- Basketball: NYU Women's Varsity Basketball Team, Center
- Basketball: NYC Urban Professional League
- Skiing: Heavenly, Lake Tahoe, Nevada
- Tennis: Central Park Tennis Courts
- Basketball and Baseball: Coach Sandy Pyonin
- Baseball: Hall of Fame, Jean Harding and Wilma Briggs

NYU Professor Karl Bardosh and Me

6. MY INSPIRATIONS:
- ISRAEL: "AM YISRAEL CHAI!" Sheep to Slaughter to Light of World!
- Rabbi David Posner, Temple Emanu-El, NYC, "President of My Fan Club"
- NYC: Personal Freedom and Creative Freedom

NYU Professor Laurin Raiken and Me

South Florida Sun-Sentinel

DELRAY BEACH NEWS   PALM BEACH COUNTY NEWS

Spirituality workshop supports A Walk on Water fund

MARCI SHATZMAN MSHATZMAN@TRIBPUB.COM | JAN 20, 2016

Sharon Esther Lampert didn't bring her tiara when she moved here from New York, but she found one just in time to be one of the speakers at Barbara M. Wolk's second annual Spirituality Workshop Jan. 24.

"Barbara has this wonderful event in support of autistic children," said Lampert, an author, poet, philosopher and educator who plays a princess for her talks.

She expects to hand out her "30 Commandments: All You Ever Need to Know," at the workshop from 10:30 a.m. to 12:30 p.m. at the Shirley & Barton Weisman Community Center, 7091 W. Atlantic Ave., in Delray Beach.

Admission is a minimum of $10 and the event opens at 10 a.m. A live auction will include a sculpture called "Balance."

EVERY THOUGHT IN YOUR HEAD WAS PUT THERE BY A WRITER
— Sharon Esther Lampert

I Am **M**ortal
My Books Are **I**mmortal
Please Handle My Books Gently
My Books Are My Remains

This book was compiled in three parts.
Part 1. Birth—Age 9-Present
Part 2. Format Book—June 29, 2022
Part 3. Publish—August 19, 2022

Sharon Esther Lampert
SEE THE WORLD THROUGH THE EYES OF A CREATIVE GENIUS
Poet, **P**rophet, **P**hilosopher, **P**eacemaker, **P**rincess & **P**ea, **Pr**o**di**g**y**

FAIR USE NOTICE
There are a few copyrighted materials whose use has not been specifically authorized by the copyright owner. We are making this material available in its efforts to advance the understanding of poetry, philosophy, spirituality, and education. We believe this constitutes a 'fair use' of the copyrighted material as provided for in Section 107 of the US Copyright Law.

www.ingramcontent.com/pod-product-compliance
Lightning Source LLC
Chambersburg PA
CBHW051348110526
44591CB00025B/2943